Embroidery for Everyone

Easy to Learn Techniques with 50 Patterns!

becker&mayer! books

Brimming with creative inspiration, how-to projects, and useful information to enrich your everyday life, Quarto Knows is a favorite destination for those pursuing their interests and passions. Visit our site and dig deeper with our books into your area of interest: Quarto Creates, Quarto Cooks, Quarto Homes, Quarto Lives, Quarto Drives, Quarto Explores, Quarto Gifts, or Quarto Kids.

Published in 2021 by becker&mayer! books, an imprint of The Quarto Group, 11120 NE 33rd Place, Suite 201, Bellevue, WA 98004 USA.
www.QuartoKnows.com

becker&mayer! books titles are also available at discount for retail, wholesale, promotional, and bulk purchase. For details, contact the Special Sales Manager by email at specialsales@quarto.com or by mail at The Quarto Group, Attn: Special Sales Manager, 100 Cummings Center Suite 265D, Beverly, MA 01915 USA.

21 22 23 24 25   5 4 3 2 1

ISBN: 978-0-7603-7223-4

Digital edition published in 2021
eISBN: 978-0-7603-7224-1

Library of Congress Cataloging-in-Publication Data available upon request.

Author: Kelly Fletcher

Printed, manufactured, and assembled in Guangdong, China, 7/21.

Image credits: All stock photographs and design elements © Shutterstock

#344001

INTRODUCTION 4
TOOLS & MATERIALS 6
STITCH GUIDE 10

Patterns
1 Smart Fox 20
2 Adorable Apple 22
3 Happy Bird 24
4 Cozy Cottage 26
5 Folk Butterfly 28
6 Friendly Fish 30
7 Embellished Flower 32
8 Jolly Snowman.................34
9 Lovely Heart....................36
10 Morning Mug 38
11 Planted Flower 40
12 Charming Raccoon 42
13 Beetle 44
14 Bumblebee......................46
15 Butterfly..........................48
16 Dandelion........................50
17 Dragonfly 52
18 Flowers & Sprigs.............54
19 Hummingbird.................56
20 Ladybug...........................58
21 Leaves 60
22 Mushrooms 62
23 Seedpods 64
24 Water Lily 66
25 Pretty Posy......................68
26 Springtime Rabbit 70

27 Ice Cream.........................72
28 Sailboat 74
29 Autumn Leaves 76
30 Pumpkin 78
31 Snowflakes 80
32 Mittens 82

Borders & Decorations
33 Raspberry Border 84
34 Blue Flower Border..........86
35 Tulip Border.....................88
36 Blue Diamond Border......90
37 Diamond...........................92
38 Feathers............................94
39 Folk Birds 96
40 Folk Flowers.....................98
41 Pocket Leaf 100
42 Circular Motif 102
43 Foliage Motif 104
44 Blue Neckline.................106

Monograms
45 Elegant Monogram..........108
46 Laurel Monogram 108
47 Floral Monogram 109
48 Grand Monogram............110
49 Rustic Monogram 111
50 Romantic Monogram......111

TEMPLATES...112
ABOUT THE AUTHOR 128

Introduction

If you're a beginner, the trick to falling in love with embroidery is simply to enjoy doing it. Everyone starts somewhere, so go easy on yourself to begin with – the more embroidery you do, the better and quicker at it you'll get and the more you'll enjoy doing it. Start small if necessary and build up to bigger projects. Switch stitches if you prefer doing one over another. And use your favorite colors. If you like the challenge of diving in at the deep end, break your design up into segments so you feel a sense of achievement as you finish each one.

If you're a more experienced stitcher, you'll already be enjoying the benefits of hand embroidery, from improved eye-hand coordination and brain activity to reduced stress and anxiety levels.

Either way, embroidery is a great way to practice mindfulness. It's also a lovely way to spend time alone, whether for an afternoon or a week. While your hands are busy, listen to an audiobook or podcast, unwind or process your thoughts, relish learning something new, or simply keep boredom and negativity at bay if you're stuck at home.

Whatever your skill level, there are a few things that make it easier to embroider. They'll improve your skills and increase your sense of satisfaction and enjoyment.

Feeling comfortable while stitching not only contributes to a better end result, it also allows you to stitch for longer stretches at a time. Try a few different places: a table, couch or armchair. Your arms need to be able to move freely and it helps to have something to rest your hoop hand against while stitching, whether a tabletop or a plump cushion on your lap.

Good light – daylight or a suitable lamp – will reduce strain on your eyes and because you can see well, your stitching will automatically be easier and neater. Try to sit in a way that keeps the strain on your neck and back to a minimum. Remember to get up, shake out your hands and stretch every now and then. If you wear glasses, take your work with you to your next appointment and ask your optometrist for advice as suitable lenses can be a big help. And if that's not enough, look for a craft magnifier (they often come as a package with craft lamps).

Most importantly, remember that hand embroidery is just that, embroidery done by hand – imperfections are part of the process and everyone's stitching will be unique to them. And if you have to unpick a little every now and then, or even begin a project over from scratch, so be it. Just get started, learn, experiment and enjoy the process.

Tools & Materials

FABRIC

When choosing fabric, look for a smooth cotton that has a tight weave and isn't too thick. The thread colors used in this book's patterns are best suited to white or light color fabrics.

Backing your embroidery fabric is optional, but tacking a piece of cotton voile or finely woven muslin fabric to the back helps stabilize your stitching and gives you the option of starting (and ending) new threads with a small double stitch through the backing fabric only.

NEEDLES

Embroidery needle: Sometimes called crewel needles, embroidery needles have a long, oval eye that can hold numerous strands of thread. They come in various sizes and your thread should pull easily through the eye, but not so much so that it slips out while you're stitching.

Milliner/straw needle: Milliners are also known as straw needles. They are the same width from eye to tip and are suited to doing French and bullion knots as they pull easily through wraps of thread.

Use the embroidery needle for all the stitches in this book other than French knots, bullion knots, and pistil stitch. For those, use the milliner/ straw needle.

HOOP

An embroidery hoop helps keeps your fabric taut and stops your work from puckering as you stitch.

Place the inner hoop on a flat surface and lay your fabric over the top with the section of the design you're about to embroider in the center. Loosen the screw on the outer hoop just enough so it slips over the fabric and sandwiches it between the inner and outer hoops, then tighten the screw. Grip your fabric on either side of the hoop and pull it taut (you want it drum tight), but take care not to distort the design when you do this. You may need to redo this last step a few times as you embroider, as the fabric might sag a bit in the hoop after stitching for a while.

Move your hoop around so you're able to work the stitches comfortably. Sometimes the embroidered stitches can become squashed or sink into the fabric. To fix this, pinch and lift stitches back into place using the nails of your thumb and forefinger, or slide your needle under the squashed sections and lift the stitches up again. You can avoid squashing knots and bullions by doing them last.

PATTERN TRANSFER TECHNIQUES

There are many ways to transfer printed patterns onto your fabric. Below are some of them.

Iron-on transfers: Iron-on transfers are printed using special ink that allows you to transfer designs onto fabric accurately using a hot iron. To use this technique, digitally scan the design from the back of the book and print it onto iron-on transfer sheets. The designs are reversed, so they will appear in the right direction on the fabric once transferred. Each design printed on iron-on transfer paper should transfer onto fabric multiple times before it fades. The longer you iron, the darker and thicker the lines will be and the fewer transfers you'll get out of each design. The ink may fade with washing, but this is not guaranteed, so be sure to embroider over all the lines.

Once you've scanned and printed the design,, cut it out from the transfer sheet and place it facedown on your fabric. Press the back firmly with a hot, dry iron for 5-to-10 seconds. You can slide the iron gently over the design if necessary, but make sure it doesn't move and transfer double lines. Raise a corner of the transfer paper to check that the design has transferred properly before lifting it off the fabric.

Other transfer techniques: A water-soluble pen is a simple way to transfer a design. Make a photocopy of the motif and tape it to a window, which will act as a light box. Tape your fabric over the design and trace with the water-soluble pen.

For fabrics that are too dark or thick to use the window/light box method, you can use water-soluble fabric stabilizer. Using carbon paper, trace the design onto the stabilizer. Adhere the stabilizer to the front of the fabric. After you have placed your fabric and stabilizer in the hoop, you will stitch through the fabric and stabilizer together and then remove the stabilizer according to the package directions.

THREADS

Cotton embroidery threads are made up of six strands twisted into one piece of thread, which you can split up into strands as needed. Cut a piece of thread about 16 inches (40 cm) long and divide it into the number of strands you need at one end, then slide a finger between the strands and down the length of the thread to separate them.

Certain stitches turn out better when the individual strands have been split apart and regrouped before use. These include back, granitos, satin, and straight stitch. For stitches such as stem, chain, and others where the individual strands aren't as visible, separating your thread into individual strands isn't always necessary.

Each project uses 6-stranded, cotton DMC embroidery floss. DMC is one of the largest brands of embroidery floss and it is available at most craft and fabric stores. The colors listed in each pattern are labeled with a corresponding DMC color code number.

When your stitches start looking thin and scraggly, your thread is likely stripped or it has become too tightly twisted. If stripped, end off and start a new piece of thread. If too tightly wound, spin your needle between your thumb and forefinger to untwist it or turn your hoop upside down and let your needle dangle until the thread has untwisted itself.

Stitching Guide

HOW TO START AND END THREADS

To prevent your embroidery stitches from coming undone, you need to secure the start and end of each thread. Ways of doing this depend on personal preference and the stitch you intend to use. For example, use a knot when the lump it may make underneath the fabric won't be visible—like when embroidering French knots. Finish off each thread as you finish stitching to secure it, and cut off any excess so it won't get tangled in your working thread.

WASTE KNOT

For this temporary knot, knot the end of your thread on the front of the fabric, and then take the thread to the back of the fabric, about 3 or 4 inches (7–10 cm) away from where you're going to make your first stitch. Bring the thread to the front again to start embroidering. When done, cut the knot off and thread away on the back as you would to finish.

DOUBLE STITCH

If you're using backing fabric, only make a small double stitch through the backing fabric underneath the section you're about to embroider. Then bring the thread to the front and begin stitching. Cut off any excess thread.

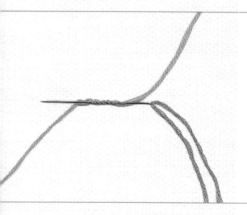

KNOT

Hold the tail end of your thread as well as the eye end of the needle between your thumb and forefinger and wrap the thread around the needle two or three times. Holding the thread taut in your other hand, pull the wraps of thread up the needle and under your thumb and forefinger, holding the eye end. Pull the needle through the loops to make a neat knot. Insert the needle directly below where you want to start to embroider.

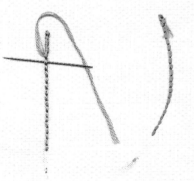

FINISHING OFF

End off a row by taking your thread to the back of the fabric and securing it under the stitching. You are, in effect, whipping the back of the stitching (see Whipped Chain Stitch on p. 13). Secure it under a few stitches (at least five, more if necessary). You can also knot the thread, keeping it as close to the back of the fabric as possible, or make a small double stitch if you've used backing fabric.

STRAIGHT STITCH

The straight stitch is also known as an isolated satin stitch or stroke stitch. This simple stitch forms the basis of many other stitches, so it's covered first.

1. Come up at A and take your needle down again at B.
2. Pull the thread through until the stitch lies neatly on top of the fabric.

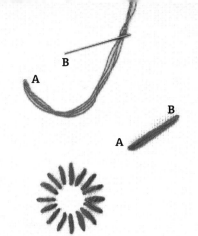

BACKSTITCH

The backstitch is good for lines and outlines, especially those with a lot of sharp points.

1. Bring the thread to the front of the fabric at A. Stick your needle into the fabric at B (the start of the line) and out again at C to create the first stitch. Continue in this way to the end of the row, using the same holes in the fabric at the start and end of each stitch.
2. To end the row, take your needle to the back of the fabric at D.

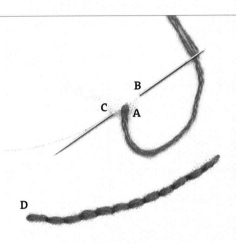

BACKSTITCH TRELLIS

To create a backstitch trellis, embroider intersecting rows of backstitch in a grid pattern in such a way that the stitches start and end at the intersections.

BLANKET STITCH

When the stitches are worked close together, blanket stitch is called buttonhole stitch. The solid line along the bottom edge of the stitches is known as the purl edge. This is a versatile stitch that was originally used to edge blankets and can be embroidered in a circle to create pinwheels.

1. Bring the thread up at A. Stick the needle into the fabric at B and reemerge at C, keeping the thread under the tip of the needle.
2. Take the needle to the back of the fabric at D to end a row, catching down the last blanket stitch.

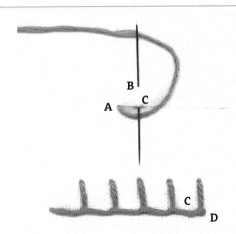

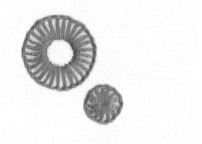

BLANKET STITCH PINWHEELS

Pinwheels can be embroidered with open or closed centers. For an open pinwheel, bring your thread up on the outer circle and insert your needle from inner to outer circle each time—keep your needle perpendicular to the lines for a neat look. For a closed pinwheel, insert your needle through the same hole in the center of the circle each time. To finish, work your last blanket stitch so it just meets the start of your first and then secure your thread with a straight stitch over the lower loop of the first blanket stitch.

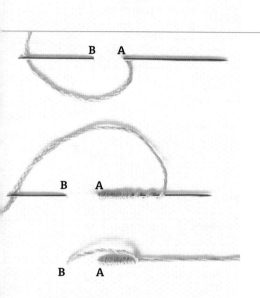

BULLION KNOT

Use a milliner/straw needle to create bullion knots. Although bullion knots can be tricky at first, once you get the hang of them, you'll find these versatile knots can be used as isolated stitches or packed together to fill an area with textured stitching

1. Bring your thread to the front of the fabric at A. Take your needle to the back at B and reemerge at A. (Take care not to split the thread.)
2. Hold the eye of the needle against the fabric with your left thumb and use your right hand to wrap the thread around the tip of the needle until the length of wound thread measures the same as the distance between A and B. Keep the wraps even but not too tight around the needle. Holding the wraps of the knot between your thumb and forefinger, pull the needle through, drawing the thread through the wraps. (If you struggle with this step, rotate your needle in the opposite direction of the wraps to loosen them or try a bigger needle.)
3. Keep pulling the thread through the wraps until the top of the knot folds back toward B. If necessary, run your needle under the wraps while pulling on the thread to even them out. Take your thread to the back of the fabric at B to secure the knot.

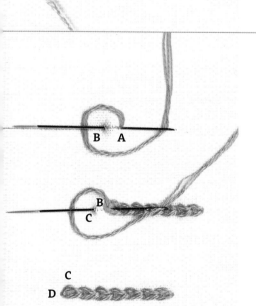

CHAIN STITCH

Chain stitch can be used for outlines as well as in rows to fill or partially fill a shape. And it can be whipped in a similar or contrasting color thread to create a new stitch.

1. Bring the thread up at A and then take your needle back down through A and reemerge at B, keeping the thread under the tip of the needle. Pull the thread through until the first chain stitch is neatly looped around the emerging thread. Be careful not to pull too tightly or the stitch will distort. For the second and consecutive chain stitches, take the needle back in at B and reemerge at C.
2. To end off a row, make a small securing stitch by taking the thread down at D. To end off a closed shape such as a circle, come up at C and then slide your needle under the top of the first chain to create a mock chain stitch before taking your thread back down through C.

DETACHED CHAIN STITCH

Detached chain stitches are simply isolated chain stitches. They can be stitched along a line or arranged in rows to fill an area of a design. They make excellent flower petals and leaves.

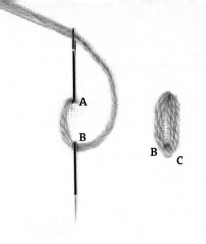

1. Bring the thread up at A and then take your needle back down through A and reemerge at B, keeping the thread under the tip of the needle. Pull the thread through until the chain stitch is neatly looped around the emerging thread. Be careful not to pull too tightly or the stitch will distort.
2. Take the thread back down at C to complete the detached chain stitch.

LAZY DAISY STITCH

Detached chain stitches arranged in a flower shape are known as lazy daisy stitches. You can keep them separate and fill the center with one or more French knots, or come up through the same hole in the center each time.

TWISTED CHAIN STITCH

Twisted chain stitch is a beautifully textured stitch and can be used to embroider a single row or to fill a shape. Keep the length of each individual stitch as consistent as possible to create a neat row of embroidery.

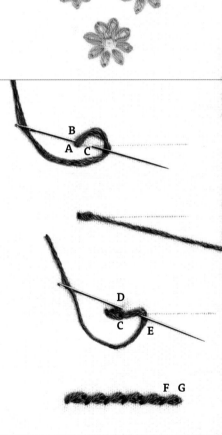

1. Bring your needle and thread up through the fabric at A. Insert your needle at B—a little to the left of A—and bring it up again on the line at C. Loop your thread around the tip of the needle. Pull the thread through to form the first twisted chain stitch.
2. Insert your needle at D, outside the first twisted chain stitch, and bring it up again on the line at E. Loop your thread around the needle tip and pull it through. Continue to the end of the row.
3. Finish with a small securing stitch over the lower edge of the last twisted chain stitch in the row, from F to G.

WHIPPED CHAIN STITCH

Bring your thread to the front at E. Slide the needle under the second chain stitch in the row, from right to left, without piercing the fabric. Whip the whole row or a section of the row of chain stitches in this way. To end off, take your thread to the back to the right of the last chain stitch.

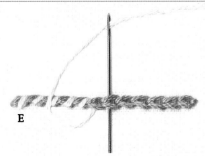

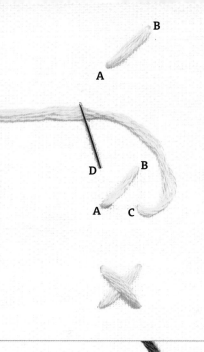

CROSS-STITCH

Cross-stitch is probably the most familiar embroidery stitch. It can be worked as an isolated stitch or in rows. The four points of each cross-stitch should form a square.

1. Bring your thread up at A and down at B to create the first half of the cross.
2. Bring the needle up at C and take it down again at D to complete the stitch.
3. Pull the thread through until the cross lies neatly on the fabric.

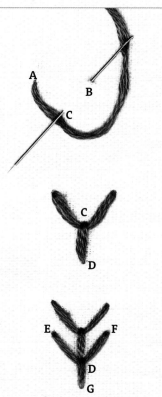

FLY STITCH

Fly stitches can be embroidered as standalone stitches or as a row of stitching. It is essentially an open detached chain stitch and is sometimes called a Y stitch because of its shape.

1. Bring your thread to the front at point A. Stick the needle into the fabric at B and reemerge at C, with the thread lying under the tip of the needle. Pull the thread through until the V of the fly stitch lies flush against the emerging thread.
2. Secure the stitch by taking your needle back down at D.
3. To stitch a row of fly stitches, bring your needle back up at E and then take a stitch from F to D as you did for the first fly stitch. Take your thread back down at G to complete the second stitch. Continue in this way to the end of the row.

FLY STITCH LEAF

Start with a straight stitch from the tip of the leaf down the central vein. Embroider a fly stitch below this, curving the V-shaped loop around the straight stitch and using a short securing stitch. Keep going as you would for a row of fly stitch, adjusting the angle and length of the V-shaped loop each time to fill the leaf shape.

FRENCH KNOT

Use a milliner/straw needle for knots. Traditionally, French knots were made by wrapping the thread around the needle just once, but today we tend to use more wraps. The French knots in this book are created by wrapping the thread around the needle twice.

1. Bring your thread up at A. Hold your needle in one hand and wrap the thread over the needle twice with the other.
2. Hold the thread taut so the wraps don't slip off the end of the needle and twist it around to stick into your fabric at B—close to A, but not through the same hole. Pull the wraps of thread taut around the needle so that they lie against the fabric and—keeping hold of your thread so the wraps don't come loose—pull your needle through to the back, drawing the thread through the loops to create the knot.

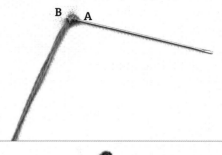

PISTIL STITCH

A pistil stitch is basically a French knot with a tail worked in the traditional way, with just one wrap of thread. Points A and B are farther apart, but the stitch is worked in the same way.

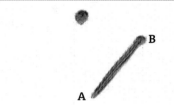

FOUR-LEGGED KNOT

This upright cross has a knot in the center. Four-legged knots can be worked as isolated stitches or scattered across an area of embroidery to fill it.

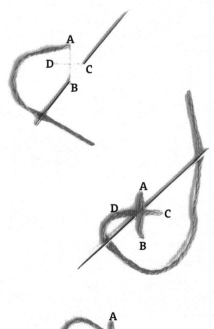

1. Bring your needle up at A, down at B, and up again at C to create the first upright stitch of the cross.
2. Lay your thread from C to D and hold it in place with your left thumb. Slide your needle under both threads in the center of the cross, from the upper right to the lower left, so your thread loops under the tip of the needle.
3. Pull the thread through gently to form the knot in the center of the cross, and take your needle down at D to finish the four-legged knot.

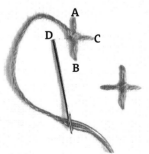

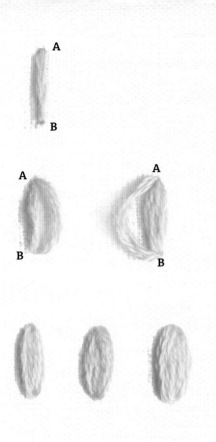

GRANITOS STITCH

Granitos or "little grains" are made up of straight stitches worked through the same holes in the fabric to create plump, wheat-kernel shapes. They work well as smaller stitches, as they retain their shape better. You can use four or five stitches instead of three to create wider granitos.

1. Bring your thread to the front at A and make a straight stitch by taking it down again at B.
2. Bring your thread up again at A and down at B, positioning it so that the second stitch lies to the right of the first. Repeat so that your third stitch lies to the left of the first. If necessary, run your needle under the stitches so they puff up into granitos.
3. Use three, four, or five stitches for each granitos.

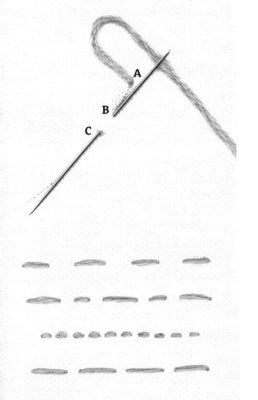

RUNNING STITCH

Running stitch is a simple stitch that can be spaced in various ways to different effect. Bear in mind when creating your own designs that sections of any line drawn onto your fabric will show, as running stitch doesn't cover the line completely.

1. Bring your thread up at A, then take your needle down at B and reemerge at C.
2. Continue in this way to the end of the row, taking your thread to the back of the fabric to complete the last stitch.
3. Experiment with different lengths of stitches and gaps to create various effects with running stitch.

RHODES STITCH

Rhodes stitch is traditionally worked as a square on evenweave fabric. But when used to fill a circle in surface embroidery, it adds a three-dimensional element.

1. Bring your thread up at A and take it down again at B to create a vertical straight stitch across the center of the circle.
2. Bring your needle up again at C and take it down at D, so this stitch crosses over the first.

3. Keep working your way around the circle like this until it is filled with thread and the center is raised where each stitch crosses over the previous one. Make sure the stitches lie across the center of the circle each time and don't slide down the side of the "dome" as it gets higher.

SATIN STITCH

Satin stitch fills an area with straight stitches. To make it easier, do it as a stab stitch: bring your thread up through the fabric and take it down in two actions. Begin in the middle of the area you want to fill and stitch outward, then return to the center and fill the other half. The shape to be filled dictates the direction of your stitches. Follow any curves by increasing the space between stitches along one edge and decreasing on the other.

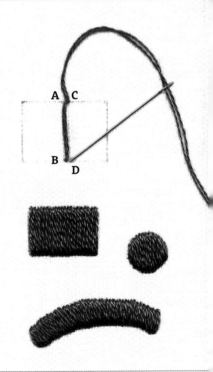

1. Bring your thread to the front of the fabric at A and take it down again at B as you would to make a straight stitch. Come up again at C and take your thread to the back again at D to create the next stitch.
2. Continue in this way until the entire area is filled with dense stitching.

PADDED SATIN STITCH

Padded satin stitch is made up of layers of satin stitching. Start with a layer that doesn't quite reach the outlines of the final shape. Then embroider another layer of satin stitch over this, filling the shape. You can use two, three, or more layers to give added height. Embroider each layer perpendicular to the last.

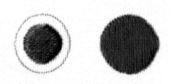

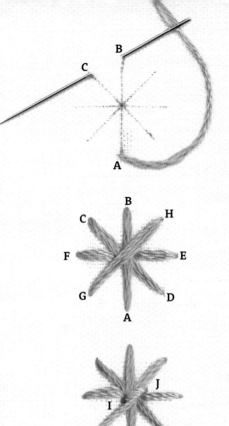

STAR STITCH

Star stitch is an isolated stitch that can be scattered randomly over an area or worked in a grid pattern for a more uniform look. It can be caught down in the middle with a small cross-stitch, too, if you prefer.

1. Come up at A. Stick your needle into the fabric at B and reemerge at C. Pull your thread through to make the first stitch.
2. Do the same from D to E and F to G, then take your thread to the back at H.
3. Complete the star stitch by catching it down with a small stitch from I to J.

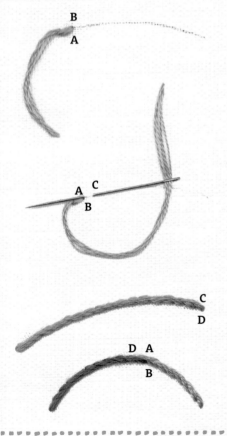

STEM STITCH

Stem stitch is good for outlines. The tricks are to bring your needle up through the hole at the end of the prior stitch and to always keep your thread below your needle. Use even stitch lengths for a neat row. Done correctly, stem stitch forms a row of backstitch on the back of your work.

1. Bring your thread up at A and, working from left to right, make the first stitch from B to A. Your thread should reemerge through the same hole at A.
2. Keep your thread below your needle at all times and make the next stitch from C to B, bringing your needle up through the same hole at B. Continue stitching along the line in this way.
3. To end off a row of stem stitch, make the last stitch from D to C and then take the needle back down at D. You can omit this last half stitch and take your needle down straight at D when making the last stitch (using this method will leave a thinner section at the end of the row). For a closed shape such as a circle, make the last stitch from A to D and then take your needle back down again at B (covering your first small stitch) to hide the join.

CABLE STEM STITCH

Cable stem stitch is done in a similar manner to stem stitch. It has a distinct look, which can be changed somewhat by adjusting the length of the individual stitches in the row. It is sometimes called cable outline stitch or alternating stem stitch.

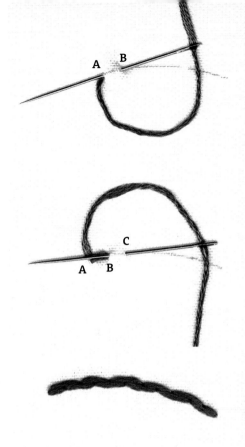

1. Working from left to right, bring your needle and thread up through the fabric at A and take your first stitch from B to A, with the thread below the needle. Your needle should reemerge at A.
2. Take your next stitch from C to B, but this time make sure your thread is lying above your needle.
3. Position your thread below your needle again for the next stitch and continue along the row in this way, with your thread alternating below and above the needle for each stitch. Take your thread down through the same hole in the fabric as your last stitch to finish the row.

WOVEN SPIDER WEB STITCH

Woven spider web stitch creates a raised circle of textured stitching.

1. Embroider a foundation of seven straight stitches radiating from the center of the circle. Take your thread down through the same hole at the center each time. Bring your thread up under one of these stitches, as close to the center as possible, and begin weaving over and under the straight stitches.
2. Continue weaving over and under the foundation stitches in an outward spiral, taking care not to pierce the fabric, until the circle is filled with thread. If you went under a foundation stitch on the previous round, go over it the next time.
3. Finish by taking your thread down under a foundation stitch, as if you're going to weave under it.

Smart Fox

| 310 Black | 907 Light Green | 727 Yellow | 699 Dark Green | 740 Orange | B5200 White |

Body

Using four strands of orange, outline the body in a double row of stem stitch and embroider the legs in backstitch.

Tail

Make the tip of the tail with stem stitch using four strands of white. Outline the rest of the tail with stem stitch using four strands of orange.

Head

Use two strands of black to satin stitch the pupils of the eyes and the nose. Outline the face in stem stitch using four strands of orange for the lower half and four strands of white for the upper half. Outline the eyes in stem stitch with two strands of orange. Fill in the ears with satin stitch using three strands of white, and outline the head in stem stitch with four strands of orange.

Background

Embroider the lines in stem stitch. Use four strands of light green for the top two rows and embroider the second line as a double row. Use four strands of dark green for the bottom two rows and stitch the fourth line as a double row. Use four strands of yellow for the cross-stitches.

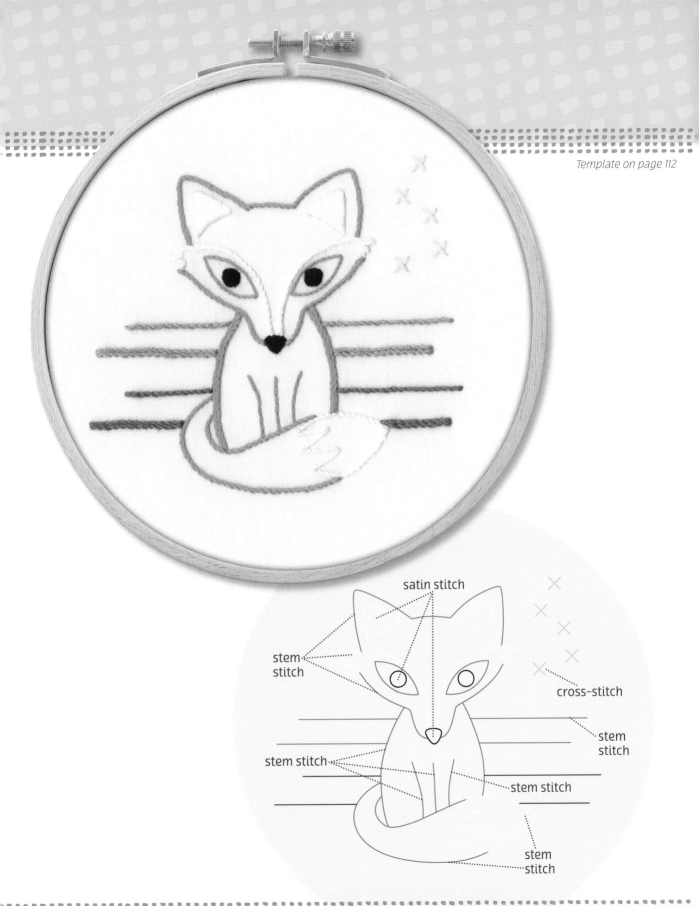

Template on page 112

satin stitch

stem
stitch

cross-stitch

stem
stitch

stem stitch

stem stitch

stem
stitch

Adorable Apple

350
Medium Coral

907
Light Green

699
Dark Green

Apple | Outline the apple in stem stitch using four strands of medium coral. Embroider a second row of stem stitch inside the first, excluding the bite. Stitch the lines on the apple in backstitch with four strands of medium coral. Embroider the crosses using four strands of light green and cross-stitch.

Stem and leaves | Embroider the stem using four strands of dark green and stem stitch. Outline the leaves in stem stitch with three strands of light green, then fill them in with detached chain stitches using three strands of dark green.

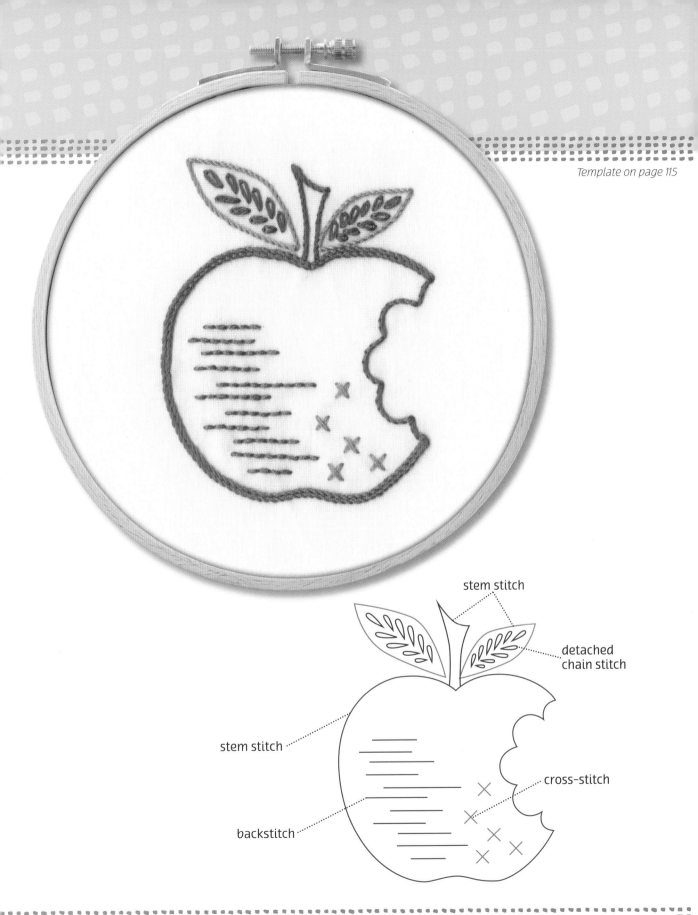

Template on page 115

stem stitch

detached
chain stitch

stem stitch

cross-stitch

backstitch

Happy Bird

761
Light Salmon

907
Light Green

727
Yellow

B5200
White

Bird

Outline the bird in stem stitch using four strands of light salmon. Embroider the wing in chain stitch with three strands of light salmon and then whip the chain stitch using two strands of white. To create the flower, use two strands of light salmon to embroider in blanket stitch and then fill the center circle with French knots using three strands of yellow. Embroider the eye using two strands of light green and satin stitch.

Background

Embroider the top of the circle in French knots using four strands of yellow. Use three strands of yellow for the star stitches. For the sprigs of foliage, stitch with four strands of light green—use stem stitch for the stem and detached chain stitch for the leaves.

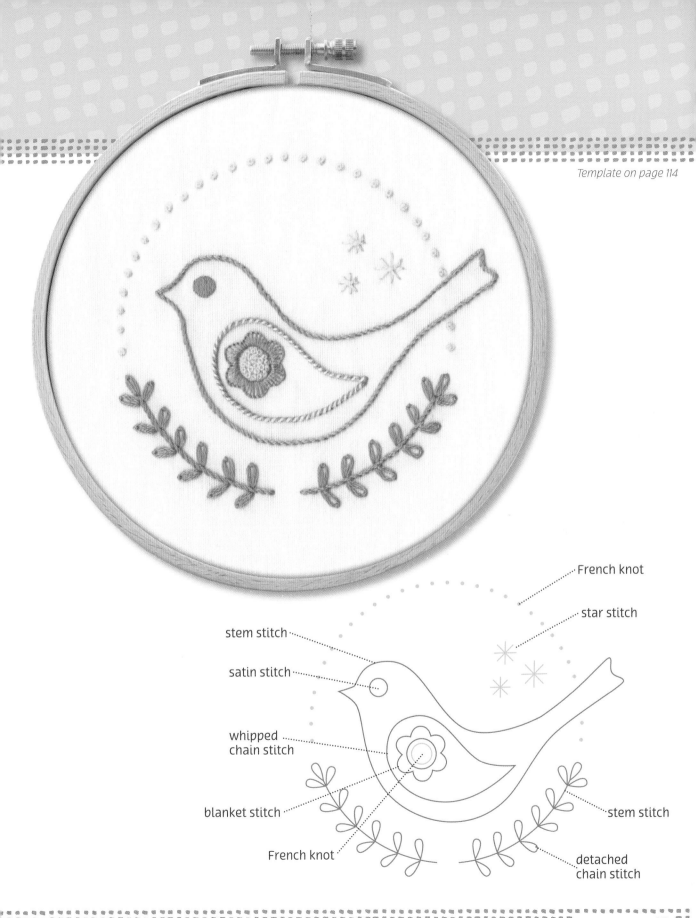

Template on page 114

French knot

star stitch

stem stitch

satin stitch

whipped
chain stitch

blanket stitch

French knot

stem stitch

detached
chain stitch

Cozy Cottage

350
Medium Coral

826
Dark Blue

827
Light Blue

907
Light Green

727
Yellow

699
Dark Green

740
Orange

B5200
White

Fence Embroider the fence posts as long straight stitches using four strands of light green. Stitch the horizontal lines with four strands of dark green in backstitch, catching the straight stitches down. Space your stitching so that there's a stitch over each post and two stitches between each pair of posts.

Sky Use two strands of thread and alternate between dark blue and light blue to embroider the satin stitch triangles.

House Outline the house in stem stitch using four strands of yellow and the window using three strands of yellow. Embroider the window crossbars with two strands of white in satin stitch. Use three strands of light green and tiny backstitches to embroider the number three, and two strands of light green in satin stitch for the doorknob. Stitch the square around the number in backstitch with three strands of dark green, then outline the door in stem stitch using four strands of dark green.

Flowers Embroider the stems with two strands of dark green in stem stitch. Working from left to right, create the first flower with detached chain stitches in three strands of white. Use two strands of orange and blanket stitch for the petals of the next flower, then fill the center with French knots using two strands of white. Create the next flower with French knots in three strands of orange. Embroider the fourth flower in the same way, but use white. Stitch the detached chain flower on the far right in two strands of orange.

Roof Embroider the lower edge of the roof in blanket stitch using two strands of salmon. Keep the purl side of the stitching along the straight edge. Outline the rest of the roof in stem stitch using four strands of salmon. Embroider the chimney with backstitch in four strands of salmon. Using four strands of salmon, stitch the French knots scattered across the roof.

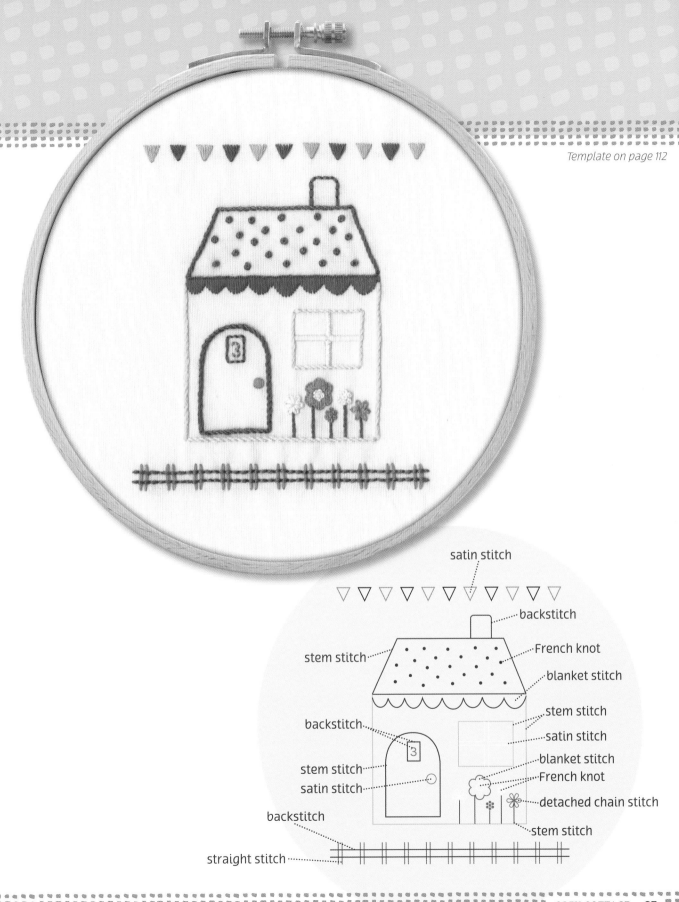

Template on page 112

satin stitch

backstitch

stem stitch

French knot

blanket stitch

backstitch

stem stitch

satin stitch

stem stitch

blanket stitch

satin stitch

French knot

detached chain stitch

backstitch

stem stitch

straight stitch

Folk Butterfly

350
Medium Coral

761
Light Salmon

826
Dark Blue

827
Light Blue

907
Light Green

727
Yellow

Body and antennae

Use three strands of light blue and straight stitch to embroider the lines on the body, then outline it in stem stitch using three strands of dark blue. Start stitching the antennae at the bottom in three strands of dark blue and backstitch, and end with a detached chain stitch.

Upper wings

Embroider the flower in the left-hand wing with blanket stitch in three strands of yellow. Make the circles in the right-hand wing in French knots using two strands of yellow for the inner circle and three strands for the outer circle. Use three strands of medium coral for the rows of fly stitch, then outline the upper wings in chain stitch with three strands of light salmon.

Lower wings

Outline the lower wings in two rows of stem stitch using four strands of light green for the inner row and three for the outer row. Stitch the smaller shape inside the wings in chain stitch using two strands of light blue. Stitch two additional rows inside the first.

Small butterflies

Embroider the left-hand butterfly in four strands of light blue. The wings are detached chain stitch and the antennae are pistil stitch. The right-hand butterfly is embroidered the same way, but using three strands of light green.

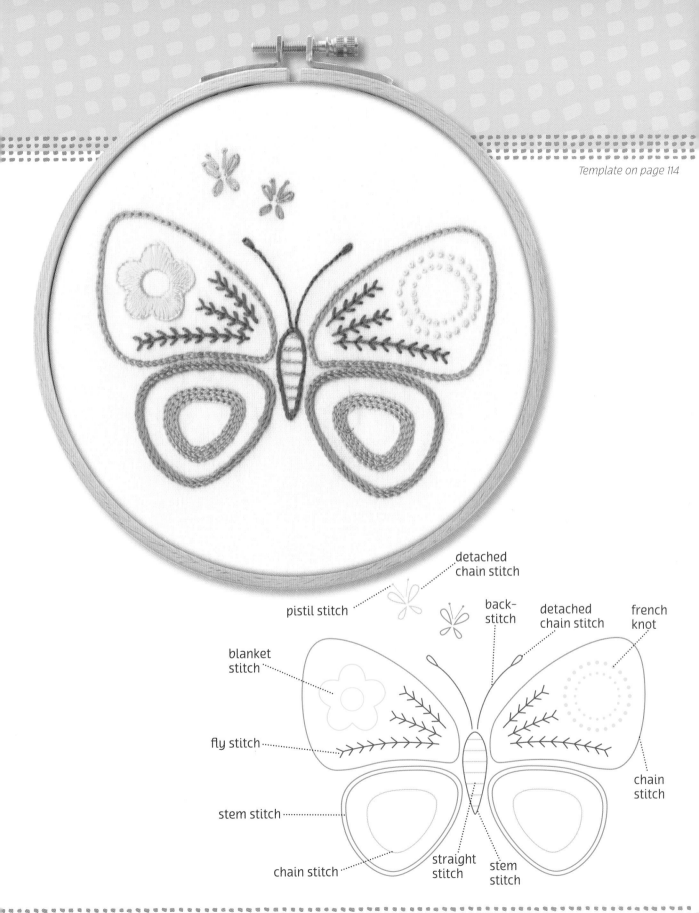

Template on page 114

detached
chain stitch

pistil stitch

back-
stitch

detached
chain stitch

french
knot

blanket
stitch

fly stitch

stem stitch

chain stitch

straight
stitch

stem
stitch

chain
stitch

PROJECT 6

Friendly Fish

310
Black

826
Dark Blue

827
Light Blue

907
Light Green

727
Yellow

699
Dark Green

B5200
White

Body

Outline the body of the fish in stem stitch using four strands of dark blue. Embroider the gills in backstitch with four strands of light blue and the eye as a blanket stitch pinwheel with an open center using two strands of black. Use four strands of dark green for the cross-stitches and three strands of light blue and star stitch to create the patterns on the fish.

Tail

Embroider the outer and inner lines with chain stitch. Use three strands of dark blue for the outer and two strands of light blue for the inner.

Fins

Outline both fins in stem stitch using four strands of light blue. Create the lines inside the fins in backstitch using three strands of dark blue.

Bubbles

The bubbles are blanket stitch pinwheels. Use two strands each of light green, yellow, and white, and the reference photo as a guide for color placement.

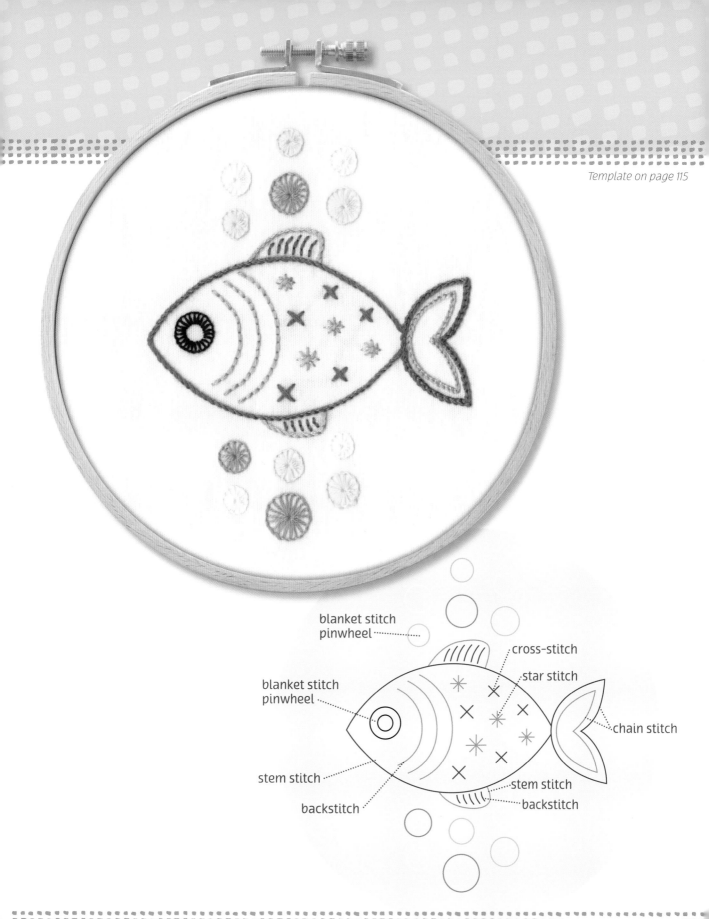

Template on page 115

blanket stitch
pinwheel

cross-stitch

star stitch

blanket stitch
pinwheel

chain stitch

stem stitch

stem stitch

backstitch

backstitch

Embellished Flower

761
Light Salmon

907
Light Green

727
Yellow

B5200
White

Inner flower

Use two strands of yellow to embroider the center circle in satin stitch. Create the petals using blanket stitch, keeping the purl edge of the stitching on the inside and using two strands of yellow.

Outer petals

Embroider the circle in stem stitch using four strands of light salmon. Stitch another row just inside the first using three strands of light salmon. Use chain stitch and three strands of light salmon for the petals. The circle in each petal is a blanket stitch pinwheel in two strands of white.

Straight stitch flowers

Use straight stitch and three strands of light green for the flower on the left and two strands for the two on the right. Use three strands of yellow for the French knots in the center of each flower.

Leaves

Outline the leaves in stem stitch using four strands of light green. Embroider the fly stitch veins in three strands of light green.

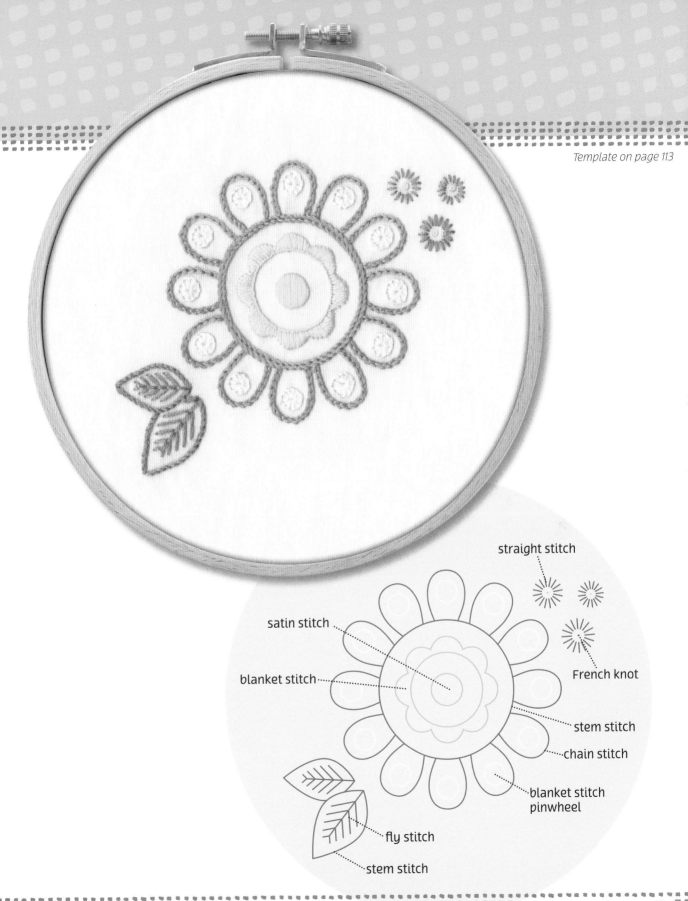

Template on page 113

straight stitch

satin stitch

blanket stitch

French knot

stem stitch

chain stitch

blanket stitch
pinwheel

fly stitch

stem stitch

Jolly Snowman

310
Black

350
Medium Coral

826
Dark Blue

827
Light Blue

907
Light Green

740
Orange

B5200
White

Snowflake	Use three strands of light blue to embroider the rows of fly stitch that make up the snowflake.
Background	Create the background lines with whipped chain stitch. Use three strands of light blue for the chain stitching and whip it with two strands of white.
Hat	Embroider the band of the hat in satin stitch with two strands of light green. Outline the hat in stem stitch in black, using three strands for the top and four strands for the brim.
Scarf	Use three strands of medium coral. Embroider the stripes in straight stitch and the outline in stem stitch.
Buttons	Embroider with satin stitch using two strands of black.
Body	Outline the snowman's body in a double row of stem stitch using four strands of white.
Arms	Embroider the twig arms in four strands of dark blue—use fly stitch for the ends of the twigs, and then carry on in backstitch for the stalks. Embroider the arm on the left over the stitching that outlines the body.
Head and face	Outline the head in stem stitch with four strands of white. Use six strands of black in French knots for the eyes. For the mouth, use three strands of black in French knots. Fill carrot nose in with satin stitch using two strands of orange, and angle the stitches to create a nice point at the end.

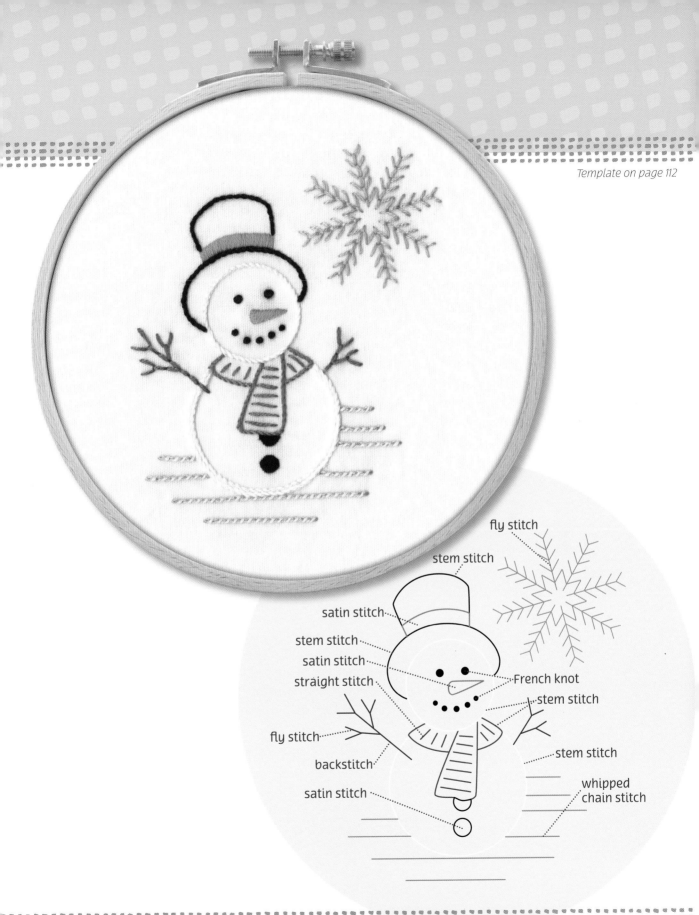

Template on page 112

fly stitch

stem stitch

satin stitch

stem stitch

satin stitch

straight stitch

French knot

stem stitch

fly stitch

stem stitch

backstitch

satin stitch

whipped
chain stitch

PROJECT 9

Lovely Heart

| 350 Medium Coral | 761 Light Salmon | 907 Light Green | 727 Yellow | 699 Dark Green | B5200 White |

Main heart
Embroider the vertical lines in backstitch using four strands of medium coral. Outline the heart in whipped chain stitch—use three strands of medium coral for the chain stitching and two strands of white for the whipping. Stitch the outer heart in stem stitch with four strands of medium coral. Embroider the circles as blanket stitch pinwheels using two strands of white.

Small heart
Outline the small heart using stem stitch with three strands of light salmon. Embroider the French knot flowers in two strands of light salmon.

Flower
Fill the center circle with satin stitch using two strands of yellow and embroider the outer circle in stem stitch with three strands of yellow. Using three strands of light green, stitch the lines inside each petal in backstitch and the background petals in stem stitch. Use four strands of dark green to stem stitch the full petals.

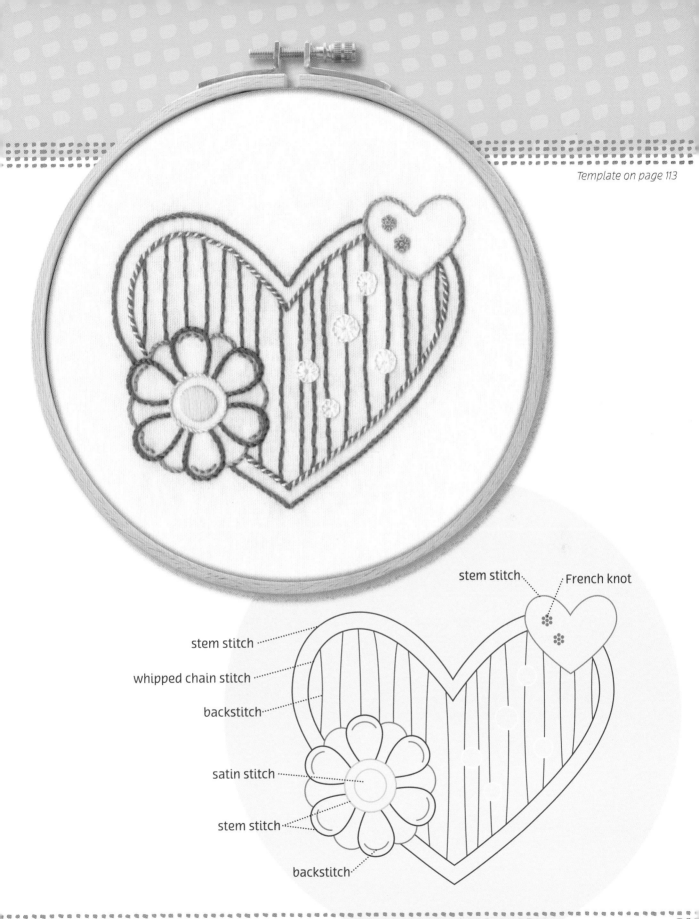

Template on page 113

stem stitch

French knot

stem stitch

whipped chain stitch

backstitch

satin stitch

stem stitch

backstitch

Morning Mug

350
Medium Coral

761
Light Salmon

826
Dark Blue

827
Light Blue

907
Light Green

727
Yellow

699
Dark Green

740
Orange

Mug

Embroider the rim of the mug in stem stitch, using two strands of light green for the inside edge and three strands of dark green for the outer edge. Outline the mug in four strands of light green in stem stitch. Use three strands for the inside edge of the handle. Create the two lines at the base of the mug using backstitch of four strands of dark green. Embroider the zigzag line in backstitch with four strands of dark blue. Stitch all three spirals of steam in stem stitch—use two strands of light blue for the left-hand spiral, three strands of light green for the middle, and two strands of dark blue for the right-hand spiral. Embroider the French knot dots on the mug using two strands of light blue.

Border

Embroider the satin stitch triangles using two strands of thread. Start with medium coral, stitch the next triangle in orange, followed by yellow, and then light salmon. Repeat the colors in this sequence all the way around the circle.

Template on page 115

stem stitch

stem stitch

backstitch

satin stitch

backstitch

French knot

Planted Flower

350
Medium Coral

907
Light Green

727
Yellow

699
Dark Green

740
Orange

Flower

Embroider a backstitch trellis in the center of the flower using four strands of yellow. Try not to split the thread at the intersections. Use two strands of orange to embroider the circles in chain stitch. Create the petals with stem stitch using four strands of salmon.

Stem and leaves

Outline the leaves in stem stitch using four strands of dark green. Embroider the central leaf vein in backstitch and the side veins in pistil stitch using four strands of dark green. Make two rows of stem stitch back to back using four strands of dark green to create the flower stem.

Background

Embroider the background in running stitch with four strands of light green.

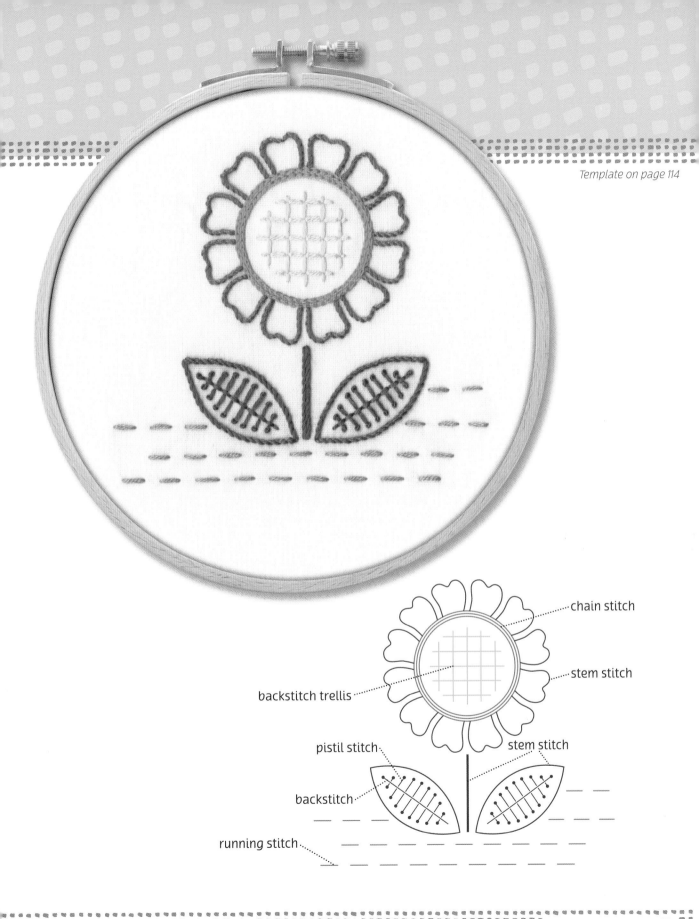

Template on page 114

chain stitch

stem stitch

backstitch trellis

pistil stitch

stem stitch

backstitch

running stitch

Charming Raccoon

310 Black	350 Medium Coral	907 Light Green	727 Yellow	B5200 White

Body

Outline the body in stem stitch using four strands of black. Make the legs with backstitch using four strands of black.

Tail

Fill each section of the tail with satin stitch using three strands and alternating between black and white. Position the stitches so they follow the curve of the tail.

Head and face

Use two strands of black and satin stitch for the nose and pupils of the eyes. Outline the eyes in three strands of black in stem stitch. Embroider the lower half of the face in stem stitch of four strands of white. Use two strands of white and satin stitch for the ears. Outline the rest of the face and head in stem stitch using four strands of black.

Border

Create the flowers using detached chain stitches in three strands of thread. Start on the lower left with salmon, then use yellow, light green, and yellow again. Repeat the sequence around the circle of flowers.

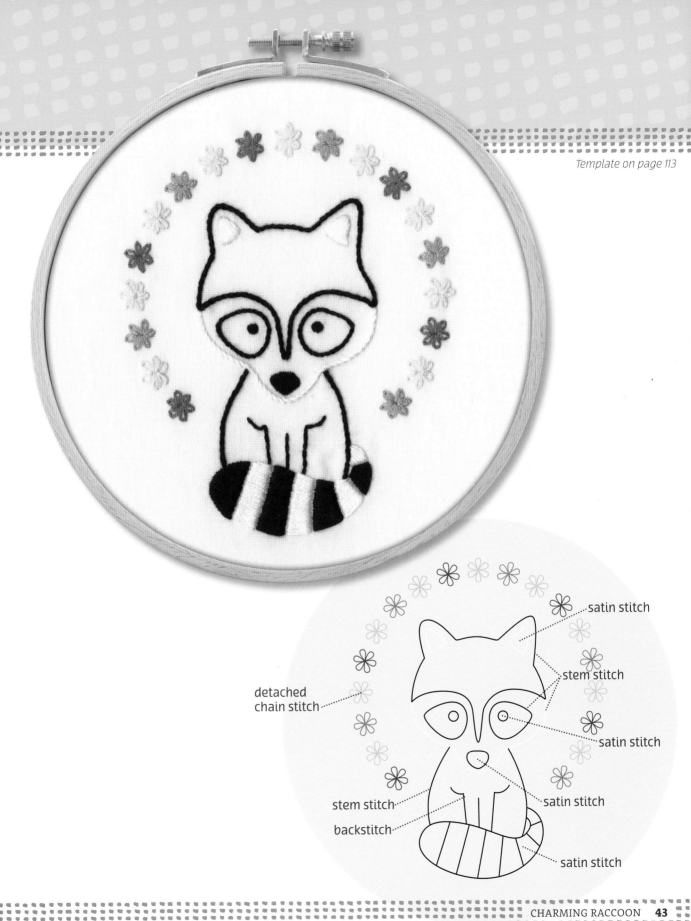

Template on page 113

satin stitch

stem stitch

satin stitch

detached
chain stitch

satin stitch

stem stitch

satin stitch

backstitch

satin stitch

PROJECT 13

Beetle

703
Green

772
Light Green

762
Silver Gray

3799
Charcoal

Body
Embroider the stripes on the beetle's abdomen in chain stitch with three strands of green thread. Then, using two strands of light green, whip roughly half of each row of chain stitch from the head down, so each row is half whipped chain stitch and half chain stitch. Embroider the patch at the neck in satin stitch with two strands of green. Outline the two upper segments of the body in stem stitch with four strands of green thread and the protruding lower segment in stem stitch with two strands of light green.

Head
Use three strands of green thread and twisted chain stitch to embroider the line on the head. Embroider the outline in stem stitch with four strands of green thread. Use two strands of light green for the French knots.

Legs
Fill the uppermost segments of the legs with satin stitch, using two strands of silver gray. Each leg is then made up of a bullion knot, a section of backstitch, two granitos made up of three stitches each, and a fly stitch at the end. Use three strands of charcoal thread. The bullion knots are long and thin, made up of 22 to 36 wraps of thread, and need to be secured in place with three or four small single stitches at intervals along the length of each bullion knot so they follow the shape of the leg. The securing stitches are worked with one strand of charcoal thread over the bullion knot so the thread blends into the wrapped thread of the knot. The middle partial leg is made up of a bullion knot with nine wraps of thread and backstitch, and the back partial leg is done in backstitch with two granitos and a fly stitch.

Antennae
Embroider each antenna in chain stitch with two strands of charcoal thread.

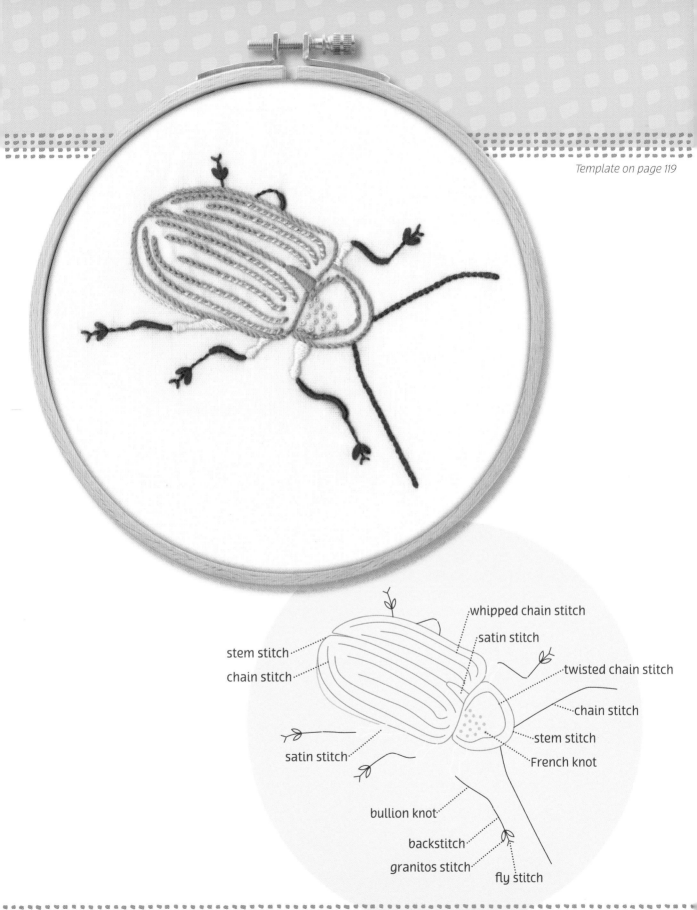

Template on page 119

whipped chain stitch

satin stitch

stem stitch

chain stitch

twisted chain stitch

chain stitch

stem stitch

French knot

satin stitch

bullion knot

backstitch

granitos stitch

fly stitch

Bumblebee

726
Yellow

3799
Charcoal

762
Silver Gray

Thorax

Outline the lower half and top of the thorax in stem stitch with four strands of charcoal thread. Fill the center spot of the thorax with satin stitch, using two strands of silver gray. Embroider the upper section in stem stitch with four strands of yellow thread.

Abdomen

The abdomen is made up of three sections, each outlined in stem stitch using four strands of thread, and with one or two rows of twisted chain stitch inside done with three strands of thread. Use yellow for the uppermost section, charcoal for the middle section, and silver gray for the lower section.

Legs

Using two strands of charcoal thread, fill the upper segments of the legs with satin stitch. Then embroider the lower sections in chain stitch and finish with two straight stitches to form a shallow inverted V.

Wings

The veins of the wings are made up of straight stitches worked through the same holes in the fabric where they meet, using two strands of silver gray. Outline the wings in stem stitch with three strands of silver gray.

Head & antennae

Use four strands of charcoal thread to outline the head in stem stitch and embroider the line across it in backstitch. The French knots are done with two strands of silver gray. Embroider the antennae in backstitch with two strands of charcoal thread.

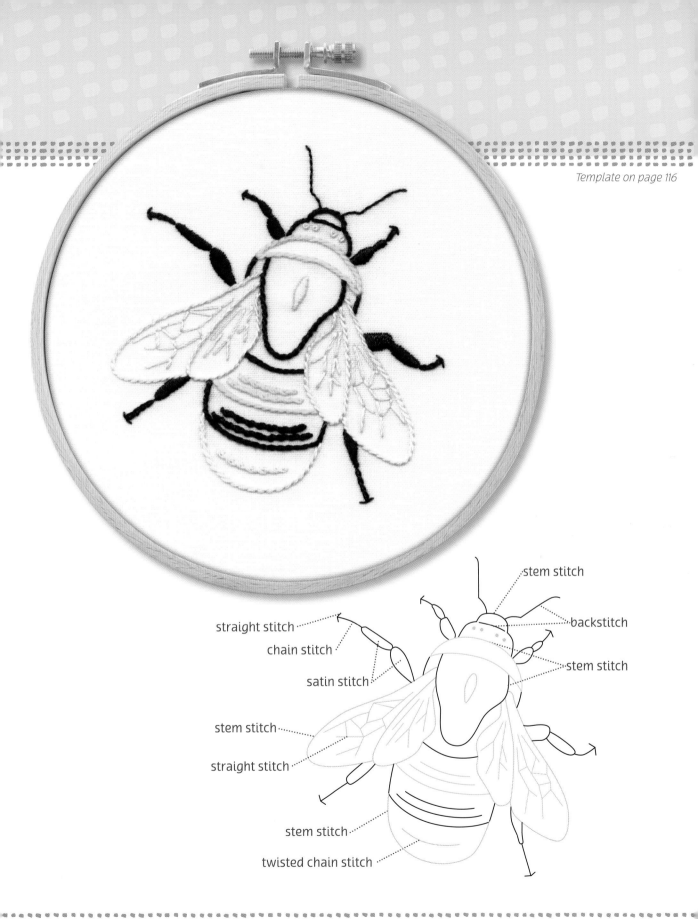

Template on page 116

straight stitch

chain stitch

satin stitch

stem stitch

straight stitch

stem stitch

twisted chain stitch

stem stitch

backstitch

stem stitch

Butterfly

| 3799 Charcoal | 798 Blue | 3811 Light Blue | 703 Green | 762 Silver Gray |

Upper wings

Embroider the center of the wings in backstitch with four strands of blue thread. Using three strands of green, stitch the line above the backstitch in fly stitch. Use two strands of silver gray to embroider the detached chain stitches above and the French knots below the rows of fly stitch. Outline the wings in chain stitch with three strands of light blue. The straight stitches along the outer and lower edges are done with three strands of charcoal thread.

Lower wings

Use backstitch and four strands of blue thread for the center of the wings. Then outline lower wings in whipped chain stitch, using three strands of light blue for the chain stitch foundation and two strands of silver gray thread to whip it. The scattered French knots are embroidered with three strands of green thread.

Head, body, & antennae

Fill the gaps between the lines on the body with satin stitch, using three strands of charcoal thread. Then embroider straight stitches over the lines with two strands of silver gray. Embroider the head in satin stitch with two strands of silver gray and the eyes in satin stitch with two strands of charcoal. The antennae are done in stem stitch with one strand of charcoal thread, with a detached chain stitch at the end of each of them.

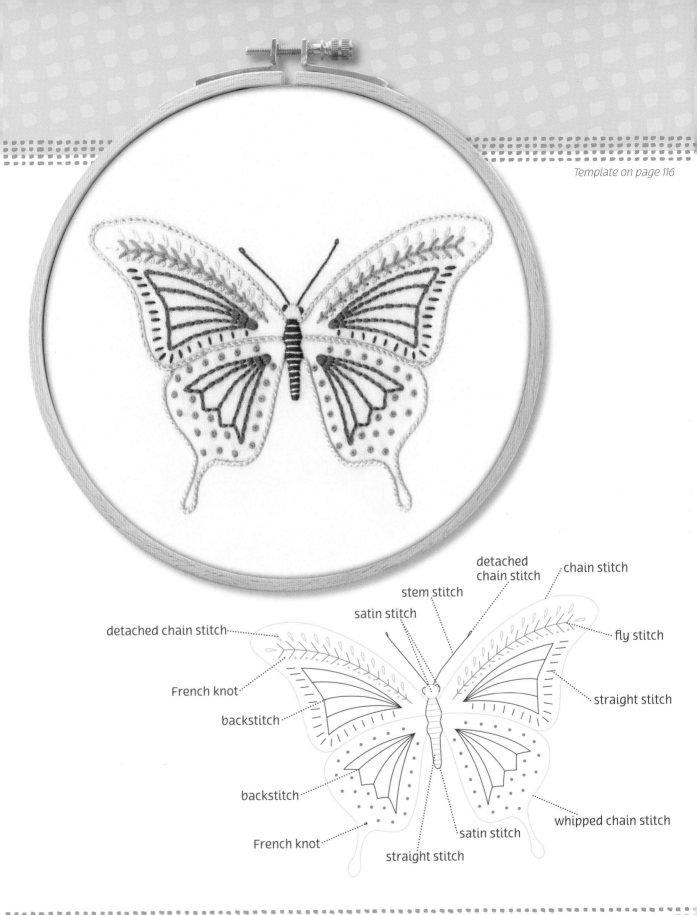

Template on page 116

detached
chain stitch

chain stitch

stem stitch

satin stitch

detached chain stitch

fly stitch

French knot

straight stitch

backstitch

backstitch

whipped chain stitch

French knot

satin stitch

straight stitch

Dandelion

772
Light Green

762
Silver Gray

726
Yellow

Leaf | Embroider the veins of the leaf in stem stitch with two strands of light green, then stitch the outline in backstitch with four strands of light green.

Dandelion | Using four strands of light green, embroider the stem in stem stitch. The center of the dandelion head is done in padded satin stitch—with three layers of stitching—using two strands of yellow thread. The seeds of the dandelion head are created using fly stitches. Embroider the inner ring of seeds with three strands of yellow thread and the outer seeds with three strands of silver gray.

Seeds | The two airborne seeds alongside the dandelion stem are embroidered with three strands of silver gray. Start at the top with straight stitches, taking your needle down through the same hole in the fabric at the base each time, then stitch the stems in backstitch and finish with a French knot at the bottom.

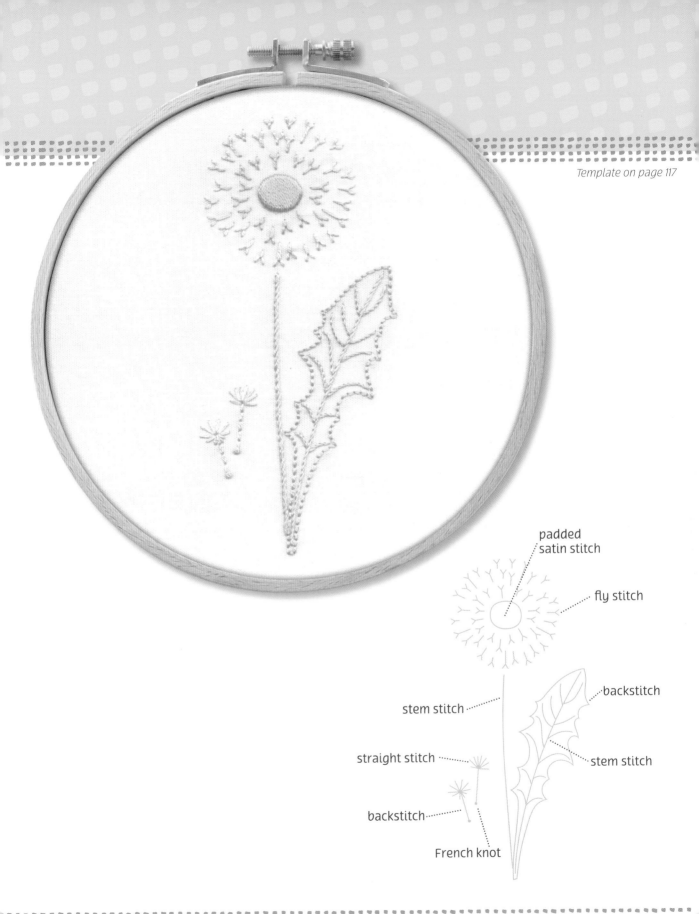

Template on page 117

padded
satin stitch

fly stitch

stem stitch

backstitch

straight stitch

stem stitch

backstitch

French knot

Dragonfly

3811
Light Blue

772
Light Green

762
Silver Gray

3799
Charcoal

Wings | Use two strands of light blue to fill the wings with straight stitches, using the same holes in the fabric where the stitches meet. Outline the wings in stem stitch with four strands of light blue.

Head, body, & legs | Although not a leaf shape, the abdomen is embroidered as you would a fly-stitch leaf. Start at the top, using three strands of light green, and follow the shape of the abdomen. The lower part of the thorax is done in satin stitch with three strands of silver gray. Embroider the eyes in satin stitch with three strands of charcoal thread and the head with three strands of silver gray and satin stitch. Fill the upper part of the thorax with French knots, using three strands of silver gray. Embroider the legs in backstitch with three strands of charcoal thread.

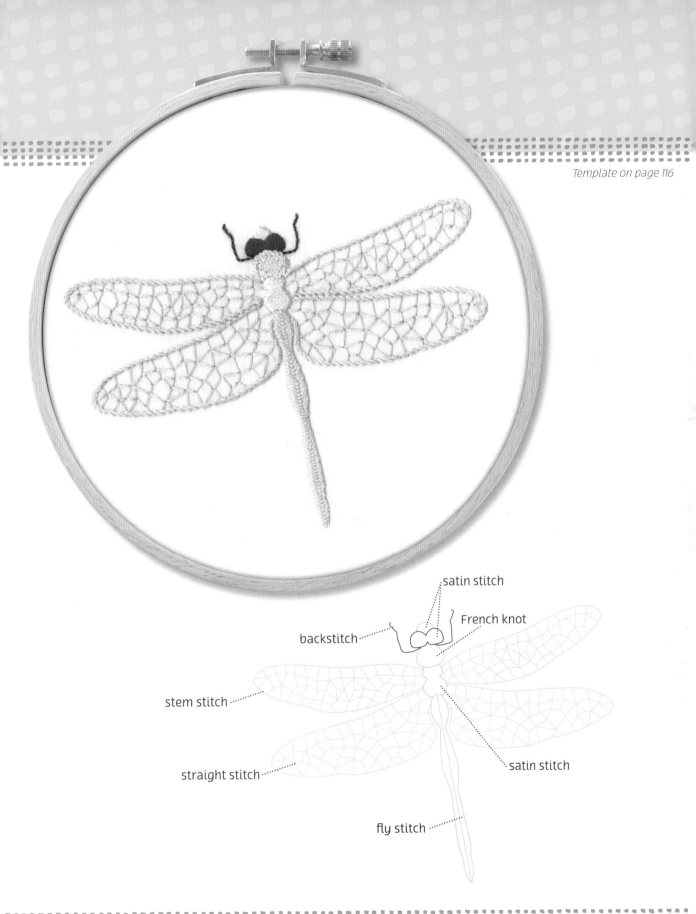

Template on page 116

satin stitch

backstitch

French knot

stem stitch

satin stitch

straight stitch

fly stitch

Flowers & Sprigs

**347
Red**

**761
Pink**

**754
Peach**

**726
Yellow**

**703
Green**

**772
Light Green**

**798
Blue**

**3811
Light Blue**

**762
Silver Gray**

Center flower	Using blue thread, outline the inner petals in stem stitch with four strands of thread and fill the solid areas with satin stitch, using two strands of blue. Embroider the outer petals in stem stitch with three strands of light blue. The flower center is made up of pistil stitches and French knots, done using three strands of light blue.
Left flower	Outline the petals in stem stitch with four strands of silver gray. Using two strands of silver gray, embroider the lines running down the petals in chain stitch and fill the base with blanket stitch so the purl edge is at the top.
Left sprig	Fill the leaves with padded satin stitch using two strands of yellow thread and two layers of stitching for each. Use four strands of yellow for the straight stitch stalk of each leaf and then embroider the stem in backstitch.
Small flowers	Fill the petals with blanket stitch using two strands of red thread. Work the individual blanket stitches close together, with the purl edge falling on the outer edge of each petal—the working is the same as for an open blanket-stitch pinwheel, just the shape is different. Fill the centers with French knots using two strands of pink thread.
Upper sprig	Embroider each small circle as a closed blanket-stitch pinwheel using two strands of peach thread.
Right sprig	Use three strands of green thread to embroider the fly stitch leaves. Embroider the stem in stem stitch with four strands of green.
Acorn	Outline the upper half of the acorn in stem stitch with three strands of green thread. Using two strands of light green, outline the lower half in stem stitch and embroider the lines in twisted chain stitch. The French knots are done using one strand of green thread.

Template on page 118

blanket stitch pinwheel

blanket stitch

French
knot

stem stitch

padded satin stitch

fly stitch

pistil
stitch

straight stitch

French
knot

stem stitch

backstitch

stem stitch

chain stitch

French knot

twisted chain stitch

blanket stitch

stem stitch

stem stitch

satin stitch

stem stitch

Hummingbird

| 347 Red | 703 Green | 3811 Light Blue | 762 Silver Gray | 3799 Charcoal |

Wings

Embroider the wings in stem stitch with three strands of thread. Use charcoal for the top three feathers of the wing on the left and top five on the right, then silver gray for the rest. Stitch the base of the right-hand wing in stem stitch with four strands of light blue.

Tail

Outline the top three feathers in stem stitch with three strands of green thread. Embroider the remaining feathers in stem stitch with three strands of silver gray.

Beak

Fill the beak with satin stitch, using two strands of charcoal thread. Start with a small stitch up from the tip of the beak and work your way towards the head, using slanted stitches.

Head

Outline the head in stem stitch with four strands of green thread. Fill the eye with satin stitch using two strands of charcoal thread and the solid area behind the eye with satin stitch using two strands of light blue. Embroider the line around the eye in backstitch with three strands of green thread.

Throat & breast

Outline the throat and breast in stem stitch with four strands of red thread. Embroider the stripes on the throat as straight stitches with two strands of red. Use two strands of red and then charcoal thread for the French knots on the breast (use red for the knots closest to the outline and charcoal for the ten outermost knots).

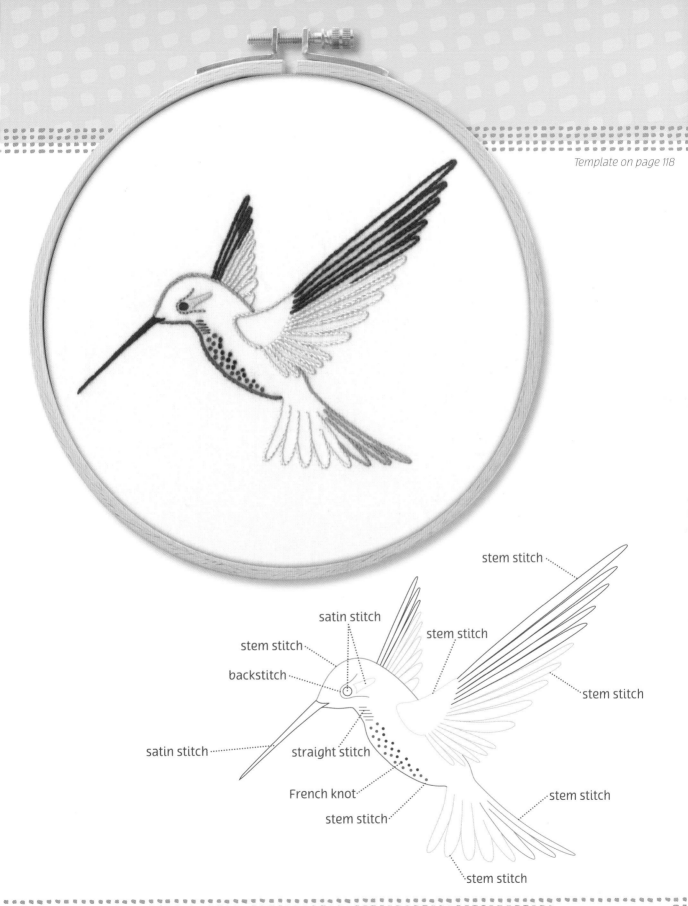

Template on page 118

stem stitch

satin stitch

stem stitch

stem stitch

backstitch

stem stitch

satin stitch

straight stitch

French knot

stem stitch

stem stitch

stem stitch

Ladybug

347
Red

3799
Charcoal

762
Silver Gray

Legs

Fill the upper sections of the legs with satin stitch, using two strands of charcoal thread. Using three strands of charcoal, start with a fly stitch at the end of each leg and embroider the rest of the lower legs in backstitch.

Pronotum

Fill the two solid areas with satin stitch, using two strands of silver gray. Outline the remainder of the pronotum in stem stitch with four strands of charcoal thread. Embroider the French knots with three strands of silver gray.

Head & antennae

For the antennae, use two strands of charcoal thread. Start with a detached chain stitch at the ends and embroider the rest in backstitch. Embroider the three lines on the head as straight stitches using three strands of charcoal thread and then outline the head in stem stitch.

Wings

Fill the dots on the wings with satin stitch, using two strands of charcoal thread. Embroider the lines in chain stitch with two strands of red thread. Outline the remainder of the wings in stem stitch with four strands of red thread.

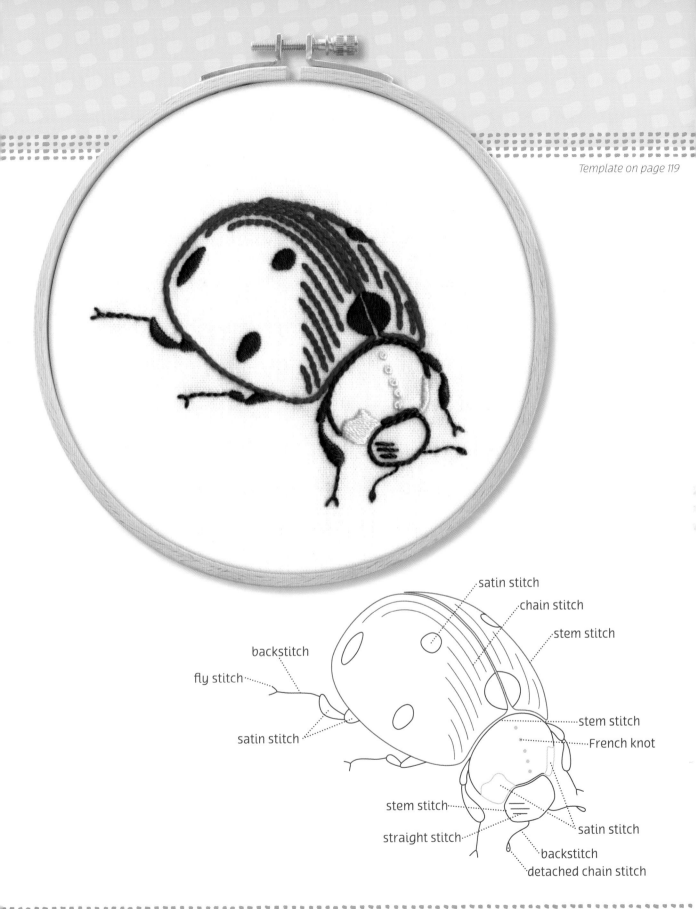

Template on page 119

satin stitch

chain stitch

stem stitch

backstitch

fly stitch

satin stitch

stem stitch

French knot

stem stitch

straight stitch

satin stitch

backstitch

detached chain stitch

Leaves

703
Green

772
Light Green

726
Yellow

3811
Light Blue

762
Silver Gray

Main leaf

Outline the leaf in backstitch with four strands of green thread. Embroider the midrib in stem stitch with four strands of green and the veins in stem stitch with three strands of green. The granitos are made up of three stitches each, using three strands of yellow thread.

Right leaf

Using three strands of light blue, outline the leaf in stem stitch, then embroider the midrib in fly stitch—the last fly stitch has a long securing stitch, which creates the stalk.

Left leaves

Use stem stitch and four strands of light green to outline the two thin leaves. The midribs are embroidered in twisted chain stitch with three strands of light green.

Lower-left leaves

Fill all three leaves with satin stitch, using two strands of green thread. Start at the apex with a straight stitch up the fatter side of each leaf and maintain the same stitch angle all the way down the leaf. End by taking your needle down through the point at the base of each leaf. Embroider the stalk of the middle leaf in stem stitch using two strands of green.

Upper-left leaves

Outline the five leaves in backstitch using four strands of silver gray. Take larger stitches than those used for the main leaf. Embroider the stalks in chain stitch, using three strands of silver gray and stitching over the backstitch outlines.

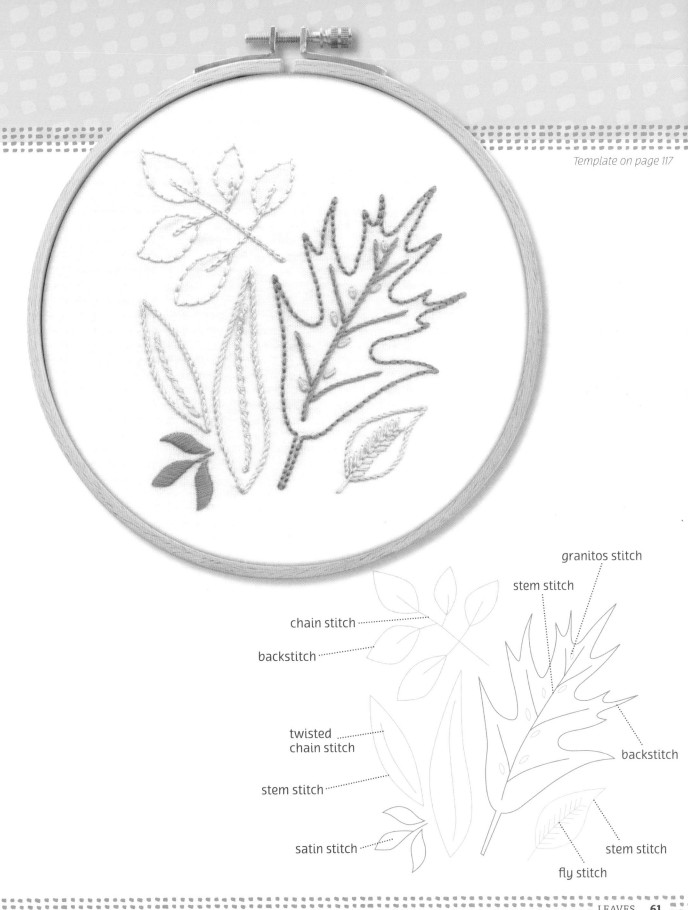

Template on page 117

granitos stitch

stem stitch

chain stitch

backstitch

backstitch

twisted chain stitch

stem stitch

stem stitch

satin stitch

fly stitch

Mushrooms

347
Red

762
Silver Gray

3799
Charcoal

703
Green

772
Light Green

798
Blue

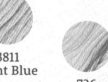

3811
Light Blue

726
Yellow

Far right   Use one strand of red thread and straight stitch to embroider the gills of the mushroom. Embroider the cap in stem stitch with red thread, using two strands for the circular lower edge and four for the upper domed section of the cap. Fill the upper half of the stalk with satin stitch, using three strands of silver gray, and outline the lower half in stem stitch with four strands. The French knots on the cap of the mushroom are done using two strands of silver gray.

Lower right   Embroider the stalk in blanket stitch down the left-hand side and then continue on with stem stitch, using two strands of charcoal thread. Use three strands of charcoal and twisted chain stitch for the lines on the cap. Using four strands of silver gray, embroider the lower circle of the cap in backstitch and the upper domed section in stem stitch.

Center   The stalks of the two mushrooms in the center are done in stem stitch with three strands of light green. Fill the solid areas on each cap with satin stitch, using two strands of light green. Using three strands of green thread, embroider the caps in stem stitch, starting with the lower circle.

Upper left   Using four strands of light blue, embroider the stalks of the two mushrooms in backstitch. Outline the caps in stem stitch with three strands of light blue and embroider the pistil stitch details last with three strands of blue thread.

Lower left   Fill the cap with satin stitch, using three strands of silver gray. Then embroider the gills and lower edge of the cap as an open blanket-stitch pinwheel with three strands of yellow thread. Start to the right of the stalk and work your way around in a counterclockwise direction. Outline the stalk in stem stitch with three strands of silver gray.

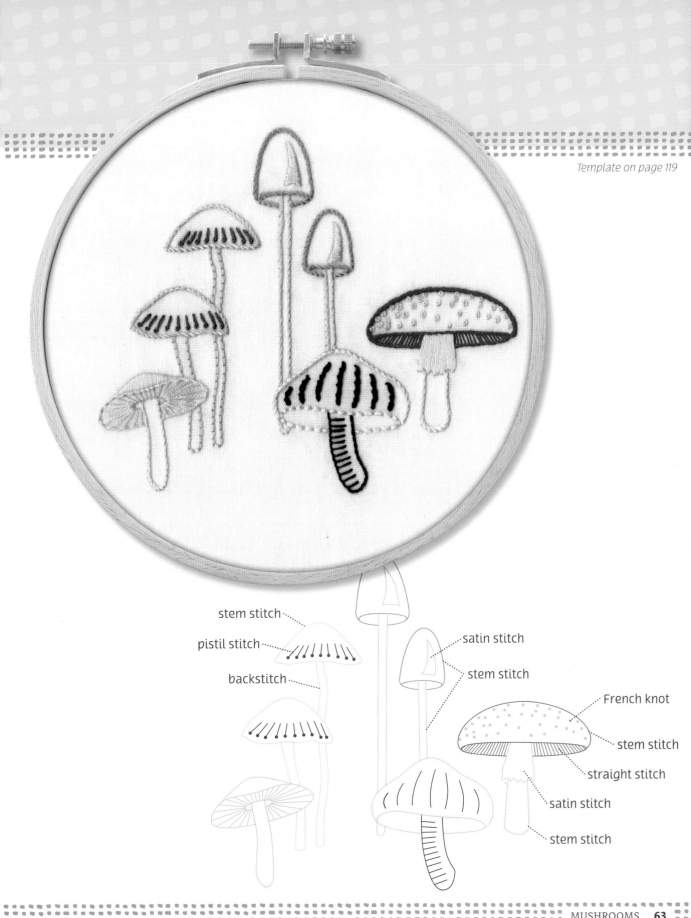

Template on page 119

stem stitch

pistil stitch

backstitch

satin stitch

stem stitch

French knot

stem stitch

straight stitch

satin stitch

stem stitch

PROJECT 23

Seedpods

 761
Pink

 754
Peach

 762
Silver Gray

 3799
Charcoal

 772
Light Green

 3811
Light Blue

Center seedpod

Fill the seeds with satin stitch, using three strands of peach thread, and outline the pod in stem stitch with four strands of peach.

Uppermost seedpod

Embroider the line down the center in twisted chain stitch with three strands of charcoal thread and outline the center section in stem stitch with two strands of silver gray. The lines at the bottom of the seedpod are done in backstitch with four strands of charcoal thread, and the seeds are embroidered as closed blanket-stitch pinwheels with two strands of silver gray. Outline the seedpod in stem stitch with four strands of silver gray.

Upper-left seedpod

Using three strands of light green, embroider the circular openings in chain stitch and outline the pods in stem stitch. Embroider the French knots with one strand of silver gray.

Lower-left seedpod

The pattern on the lower half of the seedpod is made up of straight stitches worked through the same holes in the fabric where they meet, using two strands of light blue. The pod is then outlined in stem stitch with four strands of light blue. Outline the crown in backstitch with four strands of silver gray and use long, thin bullion knots for the lines. Using two strands of light blue, create the bullion knots by wrapping the thread 25 to 40 times around the needle. Then, using one strand of light blue, secure them in place by working three or four small single stitches at intervals, along the length of each bullion knot.

Upper-right seedpod

Fill the inner segments with satin stitch, using three strands of pink thread. Outline the seedpod in stem stitch with three strands of pink. Fill the center with straight stitches, using two strands of charcoal thread. Bring your needle up on the outer edge and take it down through the same hole in the fabric at the center each time. Alternate between long and short stitches to fill the shape.

Lower-right seedpod

Using three strands of silver gray, embroider the frill with blanket stitch and the rest in stem stitch. Fill the seeds in the center with padded satin stitch, using two strands of light green.

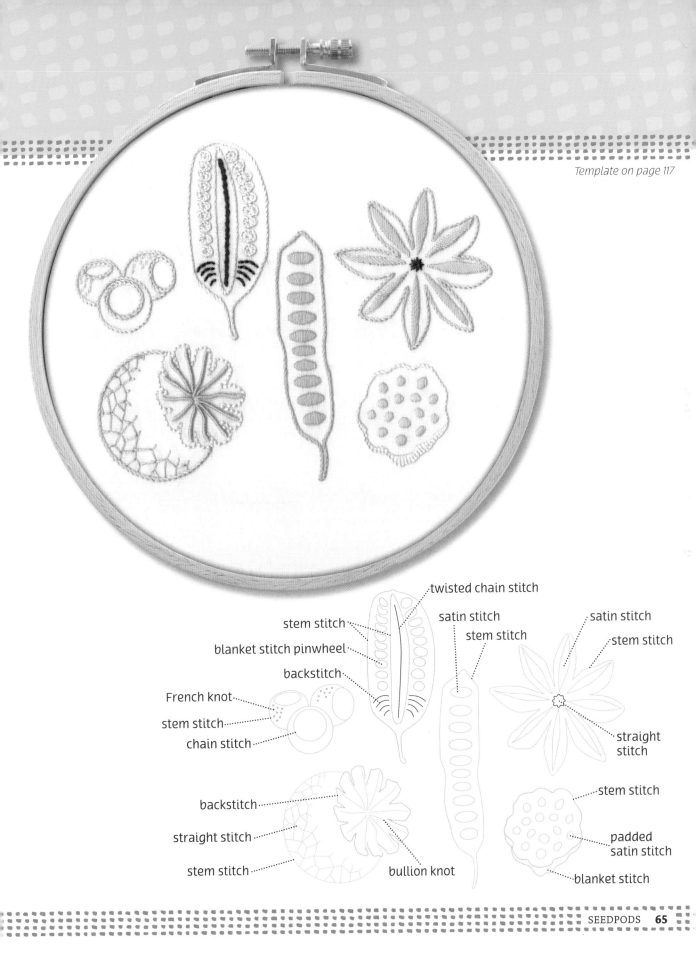

Template on page 117

twisted chain stitch

stem stitch

blanket stitch pinwheel

satin stitch

stem stitch

satin stitch

stem stitch

backstitch

French knot

stem stitch

chain stitch

straight stitch

stem stitch

backstitch

straight stitch

stem stitch

bullion knot

padded satin stitch

blanket stitch

PROJECT 24

Water Lily

761
Pink

762
Silver Gray

772
Light Green

Lily	Use stem stitch to outline the ten uppermost petals with three strands of pink thread and the rest of the petals with four strands. Embroider the lines on the petals as straight stitches with two strands of silver gray and the stamens as pistil stitches with three strands of silver gray.
Leaves	Embroider the lines on the leaves in backstitch and the outlines in stem stitch using four strands of light green.

Template on page 119

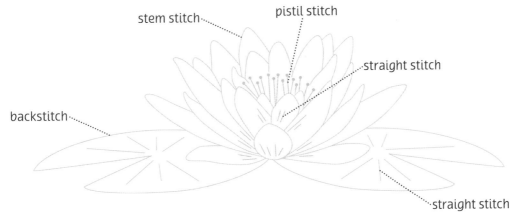

stem stitch

pistil stitch

straight stitch

backstitch

straight stitch

Pretty Posy

16
Green

445
Light Yellow

745
Yellow

772
Light Green

828
Light Blue

963
Light Pink

967
Light Orange

3747
Light Purple

B5200
White

Main flower	Embroider the stem and tendril in green using stem stitch. Use four strands of thread for the main stem and three strands for the tendril. Using light pink, outline the petals in stem stitch with four strands of thread and embroider the detached chain detail using three strands. The lower segment of the flower is done in blanket stitch with three strands of light orange and the French knot clusters are embroidered with three strands of yellow.
Branch	Use light green. Stitch the stem in backstitch using four strands of thread. The leaves are granitos made up of five stitches each, using three strands of thread.
Sprigs	The sprigs on either side of the main flower are made up of stem stitch stems using two strands and French knots using four strands of light blue.
Small flower	Using three strands of green, embroider the stem in stem stitch and the leaves as fly stitch leaves. Outline the flower in stem stitch with four strands of light purple and embroider the pistil stitches with two strands of the same color. The circle detail is done in Rhodes stitch with two strands of white.
Twig	For the twig on the left, use green. Embroider the stem in stem stitch using one strand and the detached chain leaves using two strands of thread.
Lazy daisy flowers	The little flower motifs on either side are made up of detached chain stitches arranged as a lazy daisy. Use four strands of light purple for the one on the left and three strands of light yellow for the one on the right.
Starburst	Bullion knots make up the rays of the large starburst. Use two strands of light yellow and wrap your thread around the needle between 10 and 16 times, depending on the length of the bullion knot. Use two strands of white and satin stitch for the center.
Small starbursts	The two smaller starbursts are made up of pistil stitches using three strands of light green. Bring your thread up through the same hole at the center each time.

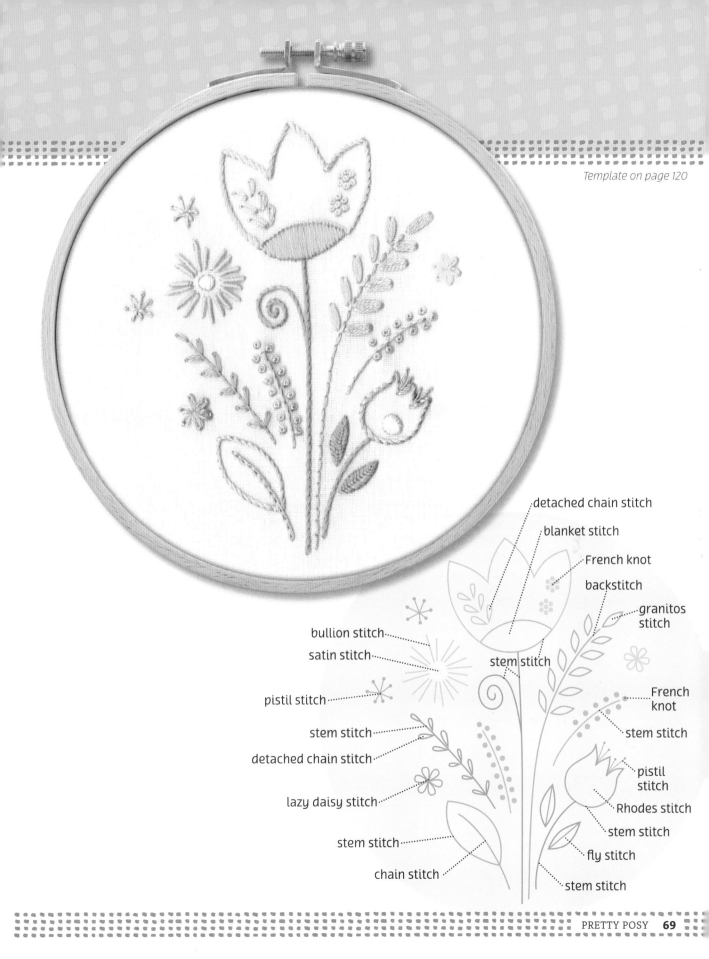

Template on page 120

detached chain stitch

blanket stitch

French knot

backstitch

granitos stitch

bullion stitch

satin stitch

stem stitch

French knot

pistil stitch

stem stitch

stem stitch

detached chain stitch

pistil stitch

lazy daisy stitch

Rhodes stitch

stem stitch

stem stitch

fly stitch

chain stitch

stem stitch

PROJECT 26

Springtime Rabbit

02
Gray

28
Purple

352
Orange

744
Yellow

772
Light Green

827
Blue

3831
Red

B5200
White

Flower Embroider the petals in blanket stitch using three strands of red. Use Rhodes stitch and two strands of yellow for the center. Using three strands of orange, embroider a row of chain stitch around the Rhodes stitch center and a row of backstitch around the circle of chain stitching to fill the gap between the petals and the center.

Leaves Using three strands of light green, embroider the veins of the leaves in fly stitch. Outline the leaves in stem stitch with two strands of light green.

Heart Fill the heart with padded satin stitch using two strands of red and three layers of stitching.

Details Fill the paisley shapes using two strands of yellow and satin stitch. Start with a stitch from the point of the paisley up the fatter side and work your way to the rounded end. Embroider the starburst using bullion knots and three strands of blue, wrapping your thread around the needle five times for each bullion. The French knot clusters are done using two strands of thread, white for the knot in the center and purple for the rest.

Rabbit Embroider the outline of the rabbit in stem stitch using four strands of gray.

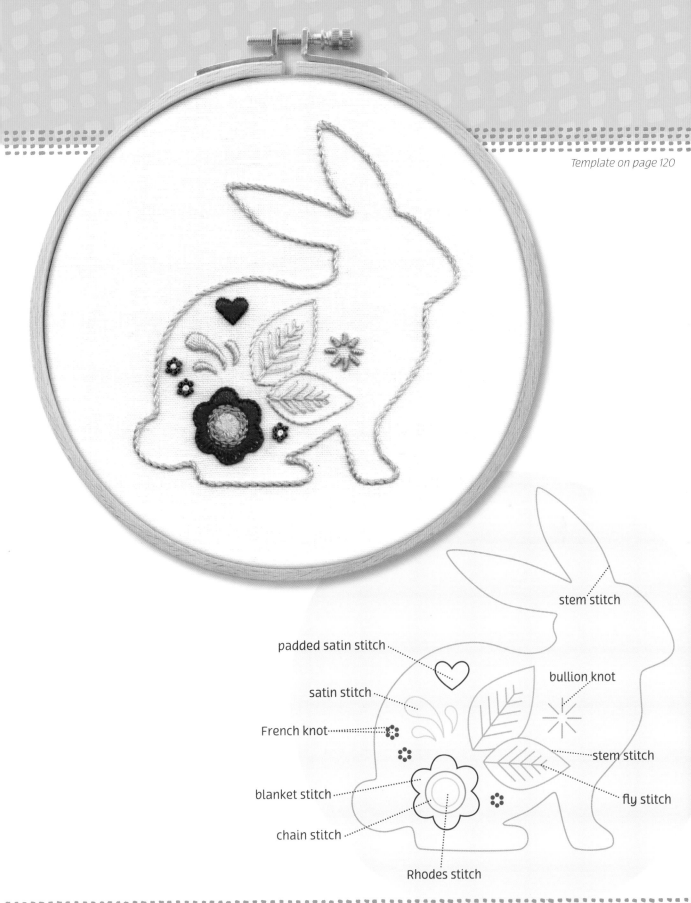

Template on page 120

stem stitch

padded satin stitch

satin stitch

bullion knot

French knot

stem stitch

blanket stitch

fly stitch

chain stitch

Rhodes stitch

PROJECT 27

Ice Cream

**15
Green**

**739
Tan**

**745
Yellow**

**761
Pink**

**841
Beige**

**842
Light Beige**

**3713
Light Pink**

**B5200
White**

Cone	Using four strands of yellow and rows of backstitch, embroider through the same holes at each intersection to form a trellis. Use stem stitch and three strands of tan at the top and bottom of the trellis. Then outline the cone in stem stitch using four strands of light beige.
Wafers	Fill the stripes with satin stitch using two strands of green. Embroider the outline in stem stitch using one strand of beige.
Ice cream	With four strands of light pink, embroider the curve in backstitch and the outline in stem stitch. Use six strands of pink and straight stitch for the sprinkles. The French knots are done in three strands of white.

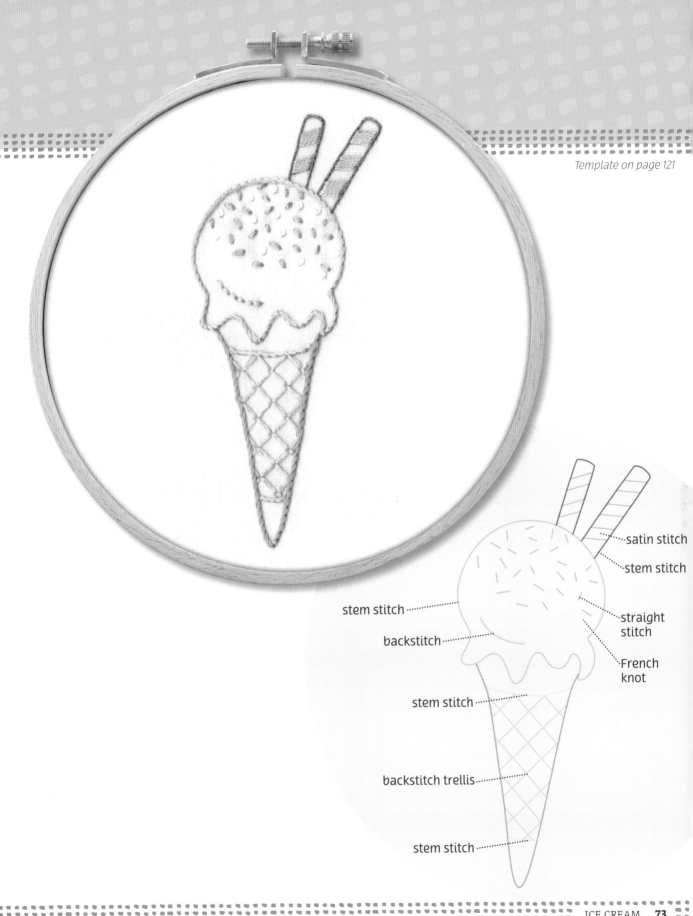

Template on page 121

satin stitch

stem stitch

stem stitch

backstitch

straight stitch

French knot

stem stitch

backstitch trellis

stem stitch

Sailboat

519
Blue

703
Green

704
Light Green

727
Yellow

762
Light Gray

3811
Light Blue

B5200
White

Sails

Embroider the two lines on the left sail using three strands of blue and running stitch. Outline the sail in stem stitch with four strands of light blue. For the right sail, use four strands of light green and backstitch for the outline and two strands of green and Rhodes stitch to fill the two circles.

Mast

Using three strands of light gray, do the mast in stem stitch. Embroider just inside the design lines so the two rows of stitching meet in the middle.

Hull

Use three strands of thread and chain stitch for the stripes on the hull: yellow for the upper, light gray for the middle and white for the lower stripe. Outline the hull in stem stitch using four strands of thread. Use yellow for the sides and light gray for the bottom of the hull, using the top stripe as a guide for where to switch colors. Outline the lip of the hull in stem stitch with four strands of yellow.

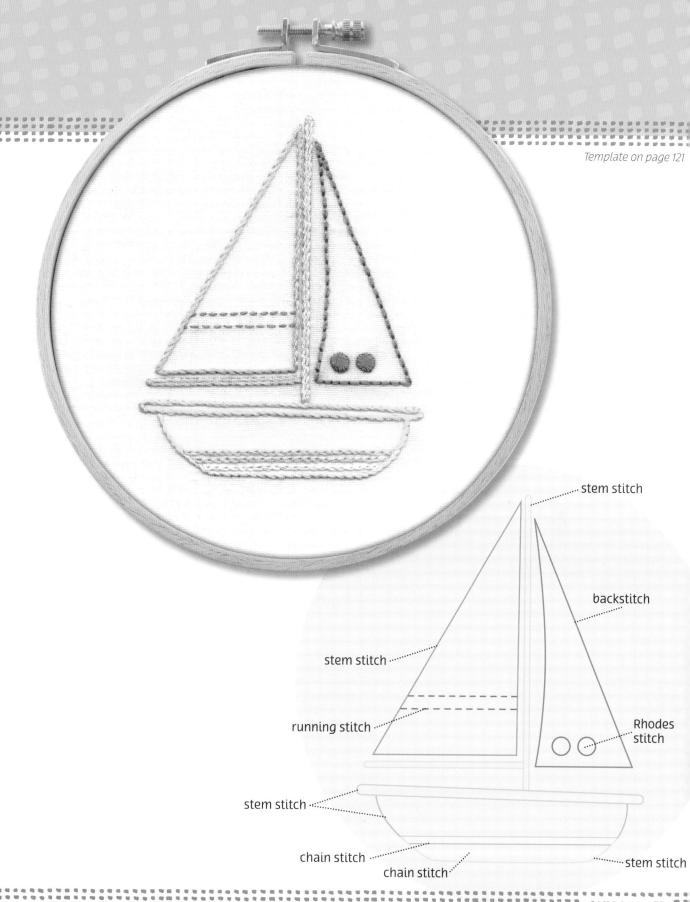

Template on page 121

stem stitch

backstitch

stem stitch

Rhodes stitch

running stitch

stem stitch

chain stitch

chain stitch

stem stitch

PROJECT 29

Autumn Leaves

12
Green

743
Yellow

754
Dusty Pink

Upper leaf | Use yellow. Fill the turned-over tip of the leaf with satin stitch using two strands of thread. Use three strands to outline the leaf in stem stitch and four strands and backstitch for the central vein and stalk.

Middle leaf | Using dusty pink, fill the turned-over tip of the leaf with satin stitch using two strands of thread. Outline the leaf in backstitch with four strands of thread. Embroider the veins in chain stitch with three strands, leaving the central vein and stalk to last.

Lower leaf | Outline the leaf in stem stitch and embroider the veins in twisted chain stitch with three strands of green. Use one strand of the same color and stem stitch for the central vein and stalk.

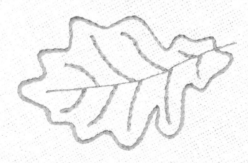

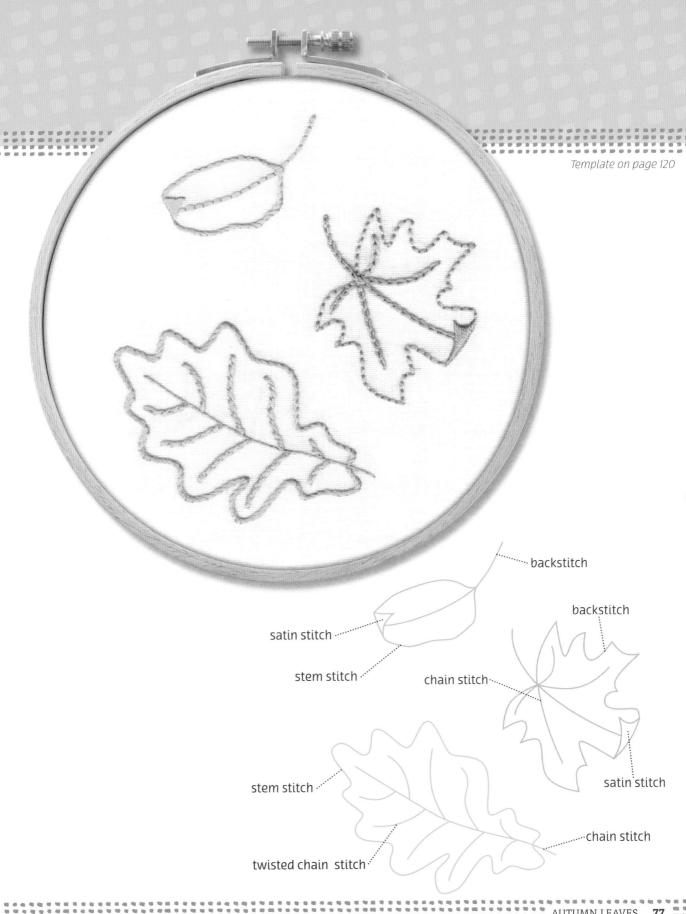

Template on page 120

backstitch

backstitch

satin stitch

stem stitch

chain stitch

satin stitch

chain stitch

stem stitch

twisted chain stitch

Pumpkin

741
Orange

905
Green

906
Light Green

972
Light Orange

Pumpkin

Outline the three main segments in stem stitch with orange, using four strands of thread for the foremost segment and three strands for the segments on either side. Use three strands of orange for the rows of running stitch and the woven spider web stitch. Outline the remaining segments in stem stitch with three strands of light orange.

Stalk

Fill the oval top of the stalk with padded satin stitch using two strands of green and two layers of stitching – pad right up to the edges of the oval to keep it flat rather than domed, but raised off the surface of the fabric. Embroider the three lines on the stalk in twisted chain stitch with two strands of green. Outline the stalk in stem stitch using four strands of green.

Tendril

Use three strands of light green and stem stitch. Embroider just inside the lines so the two rows of stitching meet in the middle.

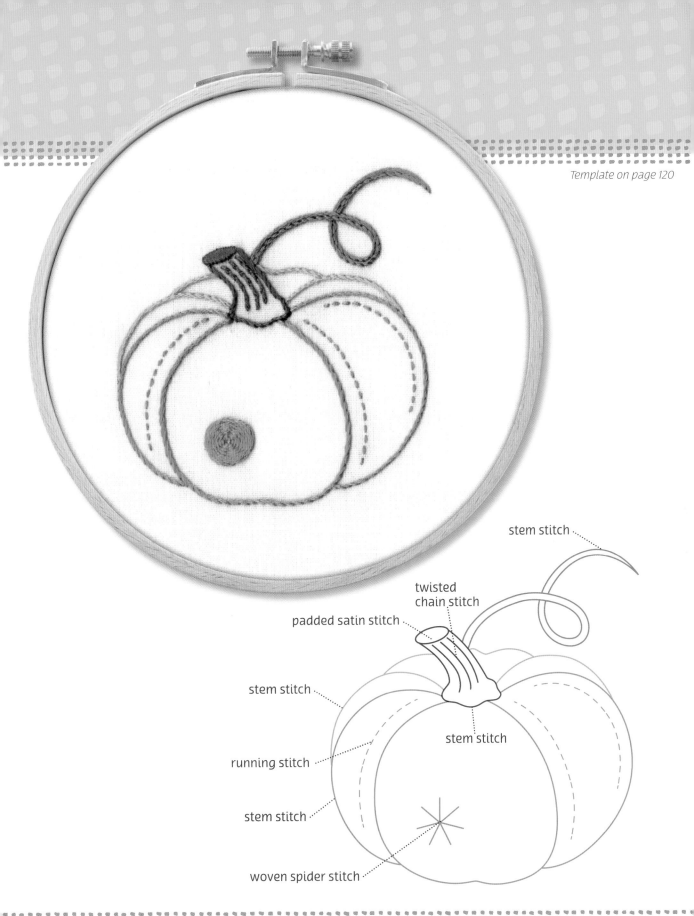

Template on page 120

stem stitch

twisted
chain stitch

padded satin stitch

stem stitch

stem stitch

running stitch

stem stitch

woven spider stitch

Snowflakes

825
Dark Blue

3761
Light Blue

B5200
White

Small snowflake

Using three strands of dark blue, start with a small straight stitch and then embroider the rest of each spike in fly stitch. Fill the center with Rhodes stitch using two strands of white.

Medium snowflake

Embroider the ribs in backstitch using four strands of light blue and then the spikes in stem stitch using two strands of the same color. Fill the circles with padded satin stitch using two strands of light blue and two layers of stitching. The French knots are done in white with three strands of thread.

Large snowflake

Use dark blue. Embroider the ribs in a jagged version of backstitch with two strands of thread. The smaller Vs at the top of the spikes are made up of straight stitches and the larger V below is embroidered in backstitch, using four strands of thread. The detached chain at the top and the backstitch length of each spike is done with three strands of thread. Switch to three strands of white and embroider a woven spider web in the center.

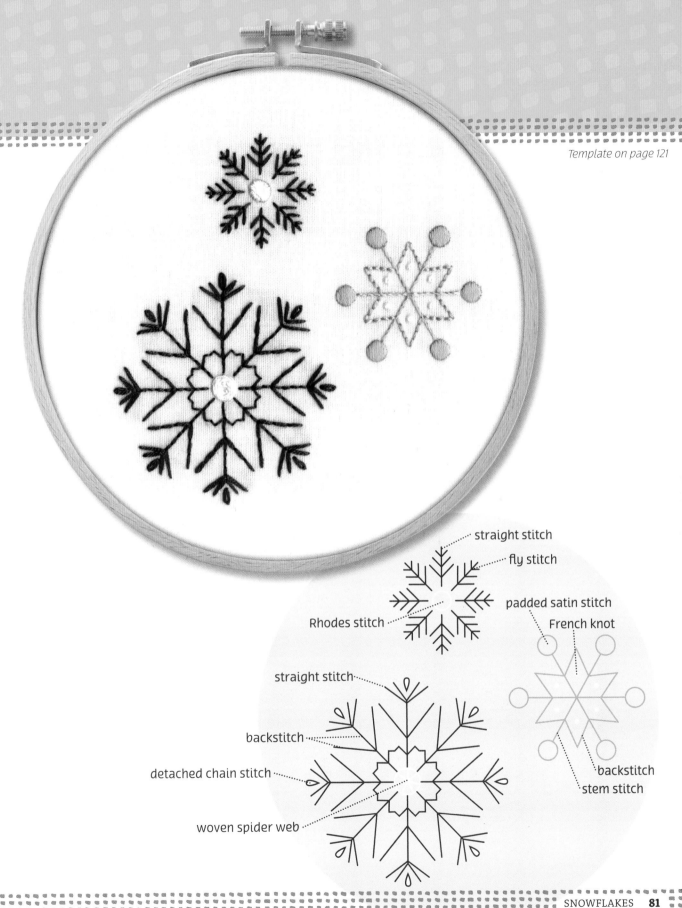

Template on page 121

straight stitch

fly stitch

padded satin stitch

French knot

Rhodes stitch

straight stitch

backstitch

backstitch

detached chain stitch

stem stitch

woven spider web

Mittens

349
Red

762
Light Gray

991
Teal

992
Light Teal

3811
Light Blue

B5200
White

Mittens

Outline the mittens in stem stitch with four strands of thread. Use teal for the cuffs and switch to light teal at the wrist line for the rest of the mittens. Embroider the wrist line in backstitch using five strands of teal. The ridges on the cuffs are bullion knots embroidered with three strands of teal. Wrap your thread around the needle 18 times for each bullion.

Details

Fill the circles at the fingertips with padded satin stitch using two strands of light gray and two layers of stitching for the smaller circles, three for the larger circles. Embroider the two lines in whipped chain stitch, using three strands of light teal for the chain stitch foundation and two strands of white to whip it. Use three strands of light blue for the star stitches and three strands of red for the row of detached chain stitches. The French knot clusters are done with two strands of thread, using white for the center knot and teal for the rest. Use three strands of light teal for the woven spider web.

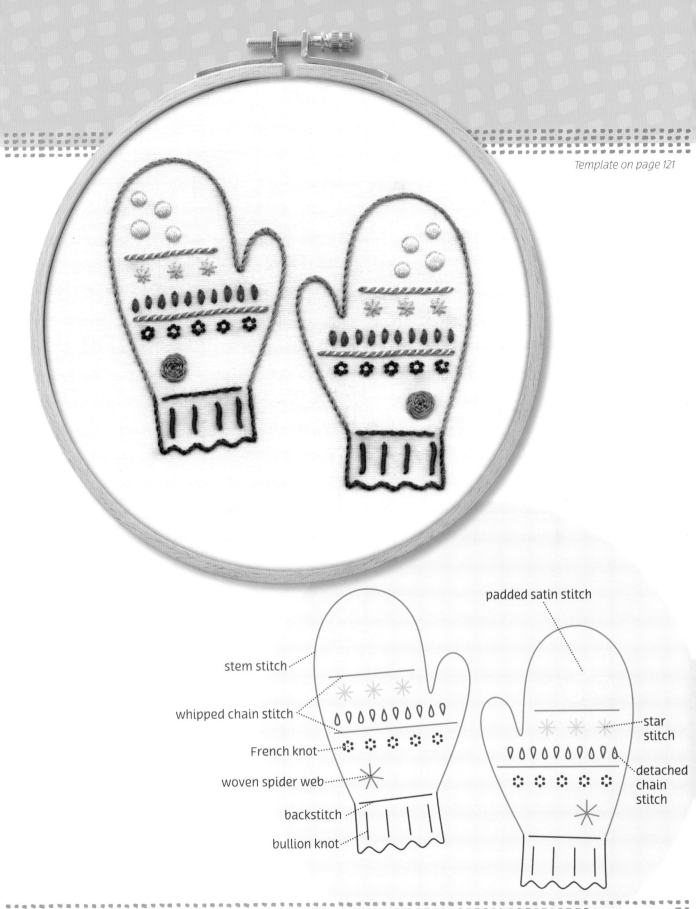

Template on page 121

padded satin stitch

stem stitch

star stitch

whipped chain stitch

French knot

detached chain stitch

woven spider web

backstitch

bullion knot

PROJECT 33

Raspberry Border

**3831
Raspberry**

**3833
Light
Raspberry**

**3777
Rust**

**B5200
White**

Outer border

Start with the scalloped edges of the design. Use three strands of raspberry to embroider straight stitches, then a row of stem stitch to create the inner edge of the border. Use two strands of light raspberry and blanket stitch to create the outer scalloped edge, keeping the purl edge of the stitching on the straight line.

Circles & details

Embroider the circles along the center of the border design as blanket-stitch pinwheels with two strands of white. The four granitos around each circle are worked using three strands of rust and three stitches for each. Depending on how the individual stitches of each granitos end up lying, you may need to add an extra stitch to create the correct shape.

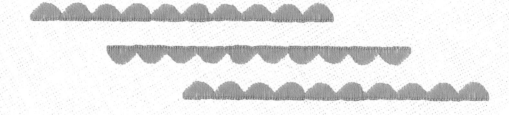

Template on page 122

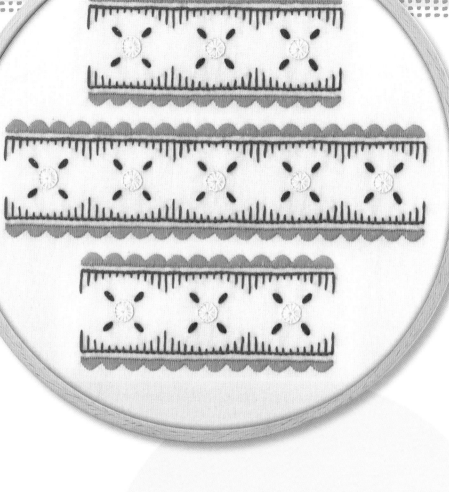

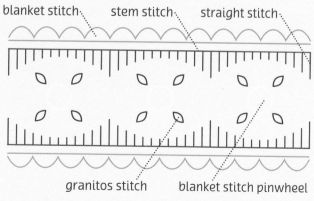

blanket stitch · · · · · · stem stitch · · · · · · straight stitch

granitos stitch · · · · · · blanket stitch pinwheel

Blue Flower Border

701
Green

704
Light Green

827
Light Blue

B5200
White

Flowers

Embroider the petals of the flowers in blanket stitch using two strands of light blue. Fill both the flower centers with satin stitch using two strands of white thread. Use one strand of light blue to embroider the stamens of the left-hand flower in pistil stitch.

Paisley

Fill the paisley shapes below the flowers with satin stitch using two strands of green. Bring your thread to the front at the pointed tip (rather than in the center) and take a small stitch up the fatter side of the paisley to determine the angle of your satin stitches, and then fill the shape from there.

Sprigs

These are embroidered in fly stitch with two strands of light green.

Lazy daisies

Use detached chain stitches and two strands of green for the small lazy daisies and two strands of white to embroider the granitos on either side. Use three stitches for each granitos.

Template on page 122

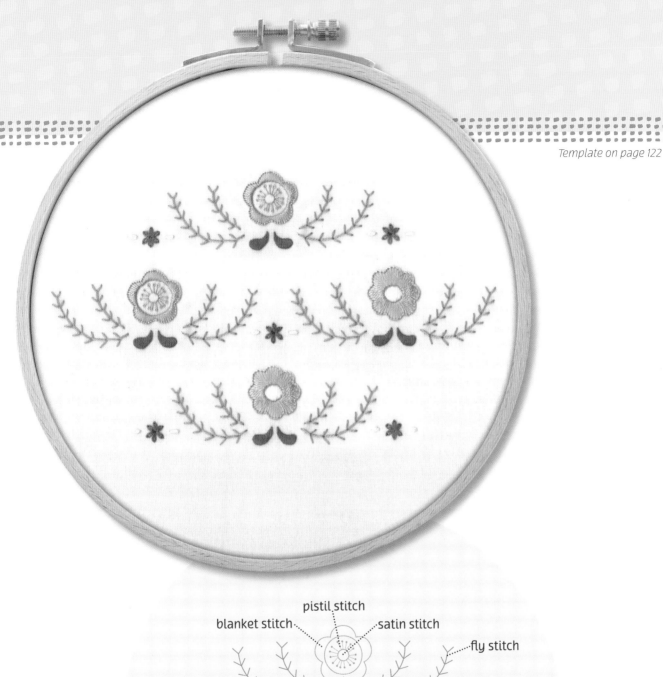

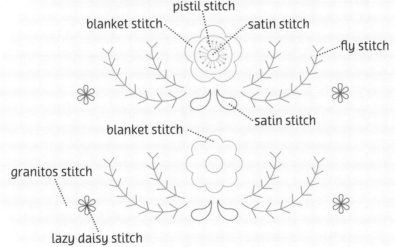

pistil stitch

blanket stitch

satin stitch

fly stitch

satin stitch

blanket stitch

granitos stitch

lazy daisy stitch

Tulip Border

 701
Green

 704
Light Green

 744
Yellow

 3831
Raspberry

 3833
Light
Raspberry

 B5200
White

Flowers Fill the center teardrop shape of the smaller tulips with satin stitch using two strands and outline the petals in backstitch with three strands of yellow. Embroider the stamens in pistil stitch using two strands of white.

Fill the center band of the larger tulips with satin stitch using two strands of light raspberry. Outline the flowers in backstitch with four strands of raspberry. Use two strands of white for the French knot in each petal.

Stems & leaves Embroider the stem of each tulip in stem stitch with two strands of light green. Use three strands of light green for the granitos leaves—three stitches for each of the smaller leaves and four for the bigger leaves.

Details The circles between each tulip are blanket-stitch pinwheels made using two strands of white.

Lines Embroider the lower line of the border in blanket stitch with two strands of green and the upper line in whipped chain stitch. Use two strands of green for the chain stitching and two strands of white to whip it.

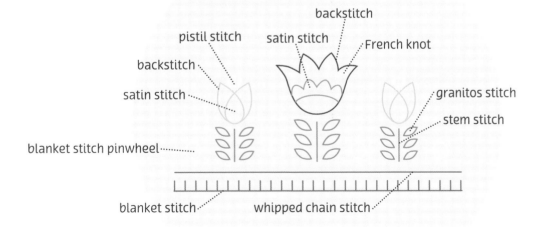

Template on page 122

backstitch

satin stitch

pistil stitch

French knot

backstitch

granitos stitch

satin stitch

stem stitch

blanket stitch pinwheel

blanket stitch

whipped chain stitch

Blue Diamond Border

825
Blue

827
Light Blue

B5200
White

Details in smaller diamonds

Embroider the diamond-shaped segments in the first and third blue flowers in satin stitch using two strands of blue. Bring your thread up at the bottom point of each segment and take it up one side of the diamond shape to begin, then angle your satin stitches as you work your way to the top of the segment to fill the shape. Use two strands of white for the French knot in the center and three strands of light blue for the four-legged knots.

Details in larger diamonds

Fill the circles in the centers of these diamonds with satin stitch using two strands of white for the center circles and two strands of blue for the outer circles. Use four strands of blue and straight stitches for the lines joining the outer circles to the middle one. Use three strands of light blue for the fly stitching in each corner of the larger diamonds; begin with a straight stitch.

Outline

Embroider each diamond in stem stitch using two strands of light blue. Use four strands of blue and stem stitch for the outer edges of the border.

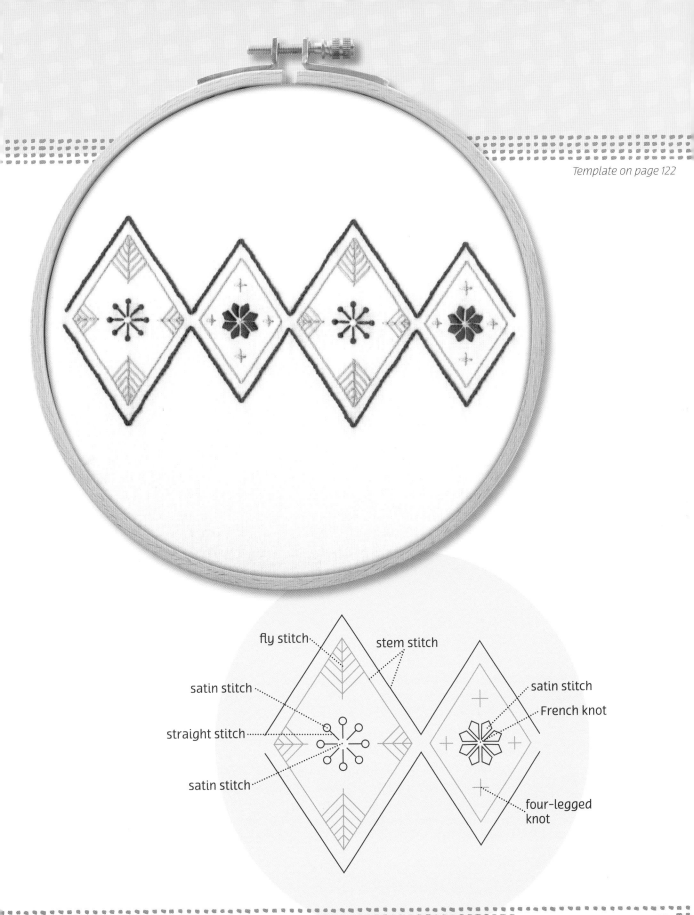

Template on page 122

fly stitch

stem stitch

satin stitch

satin stitch

straight stitch

French knot

satin stitch

four-legged knot

PROJECT 37

Diamond

701
Green

704
Light Green

741
Orange

744
Yellow

825
Blue

827
Light Blue

3831
Raspberry

3833
Light
Raspberry

3777
Rust

B5200
White

Tulips

Using two strands of yellow, outline the center in chain stitch and the two outer petals in stem stitch. Use two strands of white and three stitches for each of the granitos inside the center petal. Embroider the stem, leaves, and tendrils on either side of the tulip in light green: Use four strands and backstitch for the stem, two strands and satin stitch for the leaves, and two strands and stem stitch for the tendrils.

Embroider the two smaller tulips in backstitch using three strands of light raspberry. Use two strands of light raspberry and pistil stitches to create the starbursts inside each. The stamens are pistil stitches using one strand of white. With two strands of green, embroider the stems in stem stitch and the leaves in detached chain stitches.

Rust flower

Outline the flower in blanket stitch with two strands of rust. Work the center circle in satin stitch using two strands of raspberry and the granitos using two strands of white and four stitches to create each. Embroider the tendrils above the flower in stem stitch with two strands of green.

Orange flowers

Use three strands of orange and detached chain stitches for the bigger lazy daisy flowers. Make a French knot in the center of each with two strands of white, and embroider the stems in stem stitch with three strands of green. Use two strands of orange for the blanket stitch flowers alongside the lazy daisies.

Other details

Fill the hearts with satin stitch using two strands of raspberry. For the four small seed shapes below the tulip and the two alongside the rust flower, use satin stitch for the circles and stem stitch for the stalks in one strand of blue. The small flowers at each corner are made up of detached chain stitches in two strands of blue. Embroider starbursts scattered throughout the design with one strand of light blue and pistil stitch.

Template on page 125

stem stitch

granitos stitch

satin stitch

blanket stitch

detached chain stitch

satin stitch

stem stitch

pistil stitch

backstitch

detached chain stitch

stem stitch

blanket stitch

satin stitch

lazy daisy stitch

backstitch

French knot

granitos stitch

stem stitch

stem stitch

satin stitch

chain stitch

stem stitch

PROJECT 38

Feathers

 701 Green

 704 Light Green

 741 Orange

744 Yellow

 825 Blue

827 Light Blue

 3831 Raspberry

3777 Rust

 B5200 White

Feathers

Fill the color bands on each feather with satin stitch using two strands of thread. Begin at the shaft of the feather and stitch outward, angling your satin stitches as you go so they eventually align with the outer edge of the feather. The last stitch makes up part of the feather's outline. Use light green, orange, and yellow for the middle feather; yellow, rust, raspberry, and green for the left-hand feather; and white, blue, and light blue for the right-hand feather.

Outline each feather in backstitch using four strands of white and skipping the sections of satin stitching. Embroider the shafts of the feathers last in stem stitch using two strands of white.

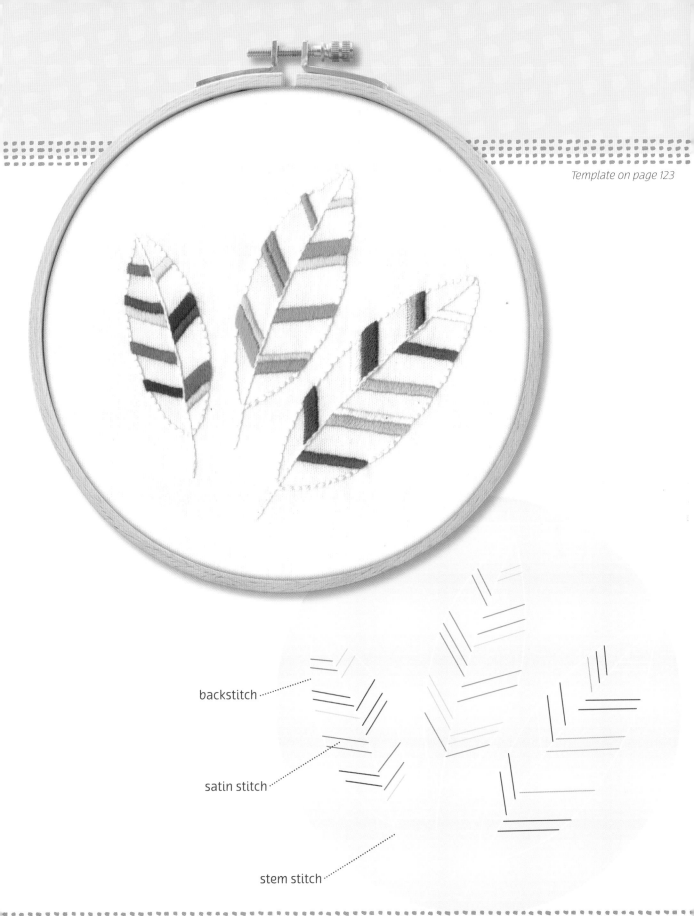

Template on page 123

backstitch

satin stitch

stem stitch

Folk Birds

744
Yellow

3777
Rust

Tail feathers — Using two strands of rust, fill the tail feathers of each bird with fly stitch and outline them in stem stitch.

Bodies — Outline the birds in stem stitch with four strands of rust.

Eyes — Embroider these as blanket-stitch pinwheels with open centers using two strands of rust.

Wings — Outline the circular wings in chain stitch with three strands of yellow. Embroider the starbursts inside each with pistil stitches using two strands of yellow.

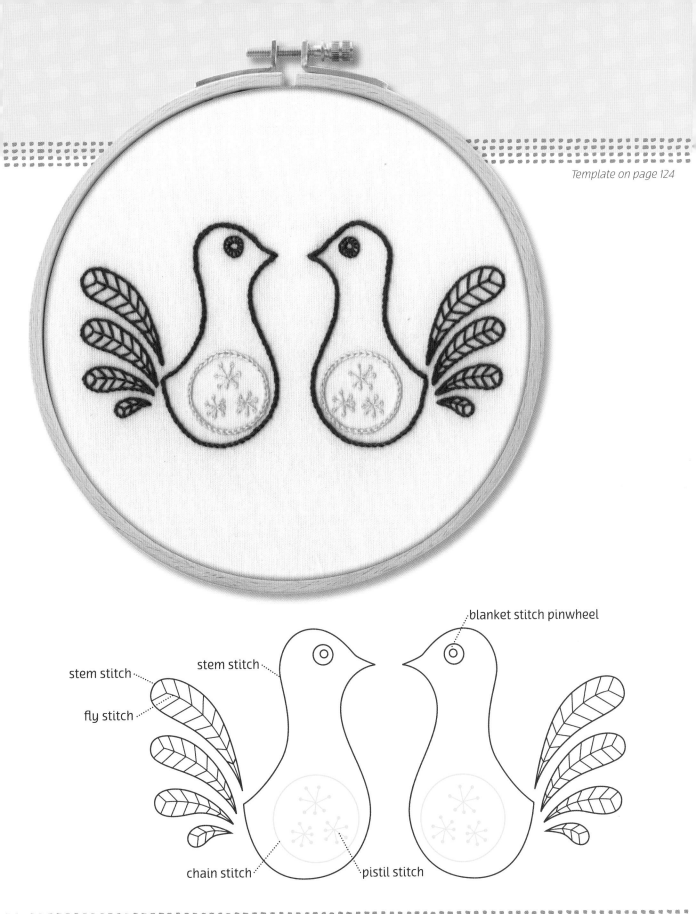

Template on page 124

blanket stitch pinwheel

stem stitch

stem stitch

fly stitch

chain stitch

pistil stitch

Folk Flowers

701
Green

744
Yellow

825
Blue

3777
Rust

Flower on left

Using rust, outline the flower in stem stitch with four strands of thread. Fill the lower section of the small flower inside with satin stitch using two strands, and then outline the petals in stem stitch with three strands of thread. Use two strands of yellow and detached chain stitches for the small petal shapes inside the flower. Embroider the stem in backstitch with four strands of green; use two strands of green and five stitches for each of the granitos leaves. The starbursts are made up of bullion knots using three strands of blue for the bigger starburst and two for the smaller one. Wrap your thread around the needle six times for each of the bigger bullions and five times for the smaller bullions.

Center flower

Outline the larger flower in stem stitch with four strands of yellow. Fill the smaller tulips inside with satin stitch using two strands of rust. With two strands of yellow, make the stamens with pistil stitch. Use green for the stems and leaves: Embroider the stems in backstitch with four strands and the leaves as detached chain stitches with two strands.

Flower on right

Embroider the outline of the flower in stem stitch using four strands of blue. Fill the circles above the flower with satin stitch using two strands of green, and the paisley shapes inside the flower in satin stitch using two strands of yellow, rust, and blue. For the paisley shapes, bring your thread to the front at the pointed tip (rather than in the center) and take a small stitch up the fatter side of the paisley to determine the angle of your satin stitches, then fill the shape from there.

Stems

For all three flowers, chain stitch the stems with three strands of green.

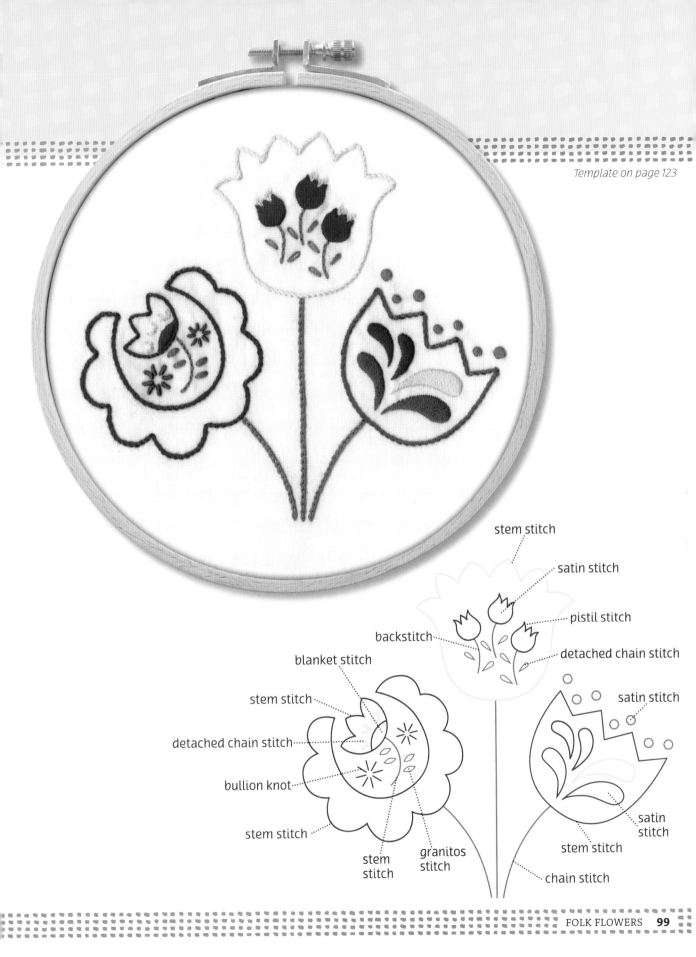

Template on page 123

stem stitch

satin stitch

pistil stitch

backstitch

detached chain stitch

blanket stitch

stem stitch

satin stitch

detached chain stitch

bullion knot

stem stitch

stem stitch

granitos stitch

satin stitch

stem stitch

chain stitch

Pocket Leaf

701
Green

B5200
White

Leaves Outline the leaves in stem stitch using four strands of green. Embroider the lines inside as straight stitches with four strands of white and then outline the shapes in stem stitch with two strands of green.

Circles Embroider the outline in whipped chain stitch, using two strands of white for the chain stitching and two strands of green to whip it. Use three strands of green and detached chain stitches for the lazy daisies inside each circle.

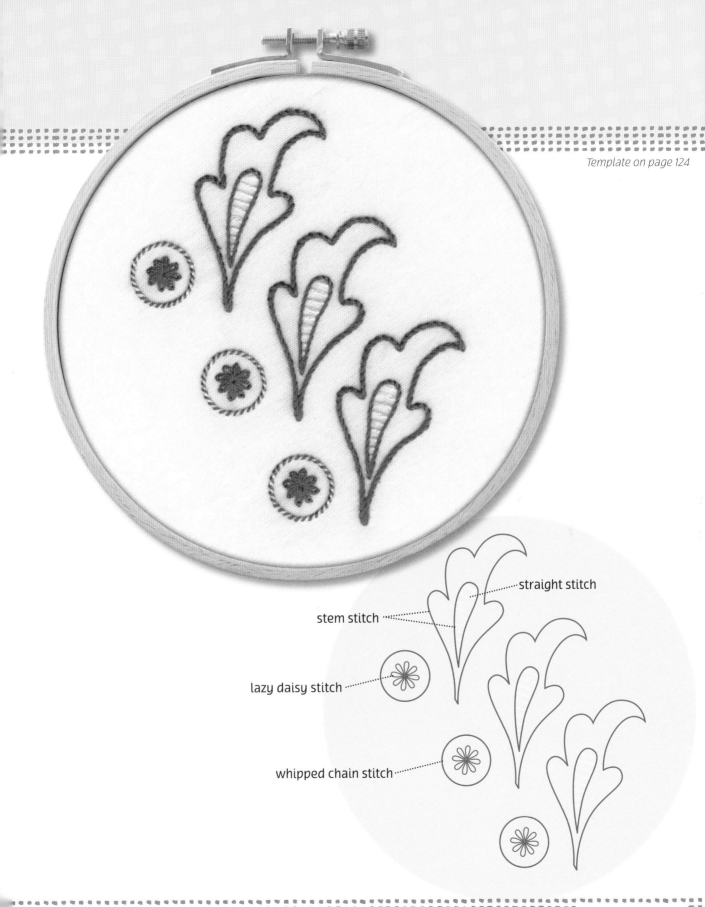

Template on page 124

straight stitch

stem stitch

lazy daisy stitch

whipped chain stitch

PROJECT 42
Circular Motif

 741 Orange
 744 Yellow
 3831 Raspberry
 3833 Light Raspberry
 B5200 White

Flower

Fill the petals of the flower in the center of the circle with satin stitch using two strands of raspberry. Take your first stitch from the point of each petal to the middle of the curve below, and first embroider one half of the petal, then the other.

Circles

Using three strands of light raspberry, embroider the two inner circles in chain stitch and the outer circle in blanket stitch.

Embroider the circle of detached chain stitches with three strands of orange.

Use three strands of yellow to embroider the circle of fly stitches and two strands of yellow for the French knot in the Y of every second fly stitch.

Fill the small circles around the outside edge with satin stitch using two strands of white.

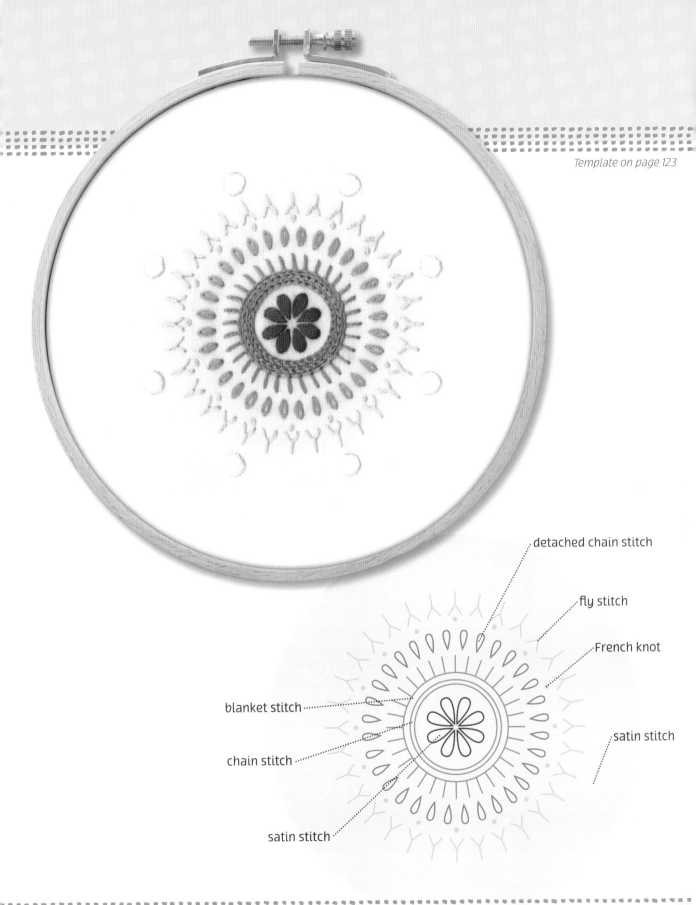

Template on page 123

detached chain stitch

fly stitch

French knot

blanket stitch

satin stitch

chain stitch

satin stitch

Foliage Motif

701
Green

704
Light Green

744
Yellow

825
Blue

827
Light Blue

3831
Raspberry

Center flower
Embroider in satin stitch with two strands of thread. Use yellow for the center and raspberry for the petals. Bring your thread up at the point of a petal and take a small straight stitch up one side to set the direction of your satin stitches, then fill the petal, keeping each stitch at the same angle. End by taking your thread back down at the opposite point.

Sprigs
Using two strands of green, embroider the two sprigs of foliage in the middle of each grouping using stem stitch for the stem and detached chain stitches for the leaves. The sprigs on either side are worked in fly stitch with three strands of light green. Use light blue for the outer sprigs: Embroider the stems in stem stitch using one strand of thread and the French knots using two strands of thread.

Starbursts
Create these with bullion knots using three strands of blue. Wrap your thread around the needle five times for each bullion.

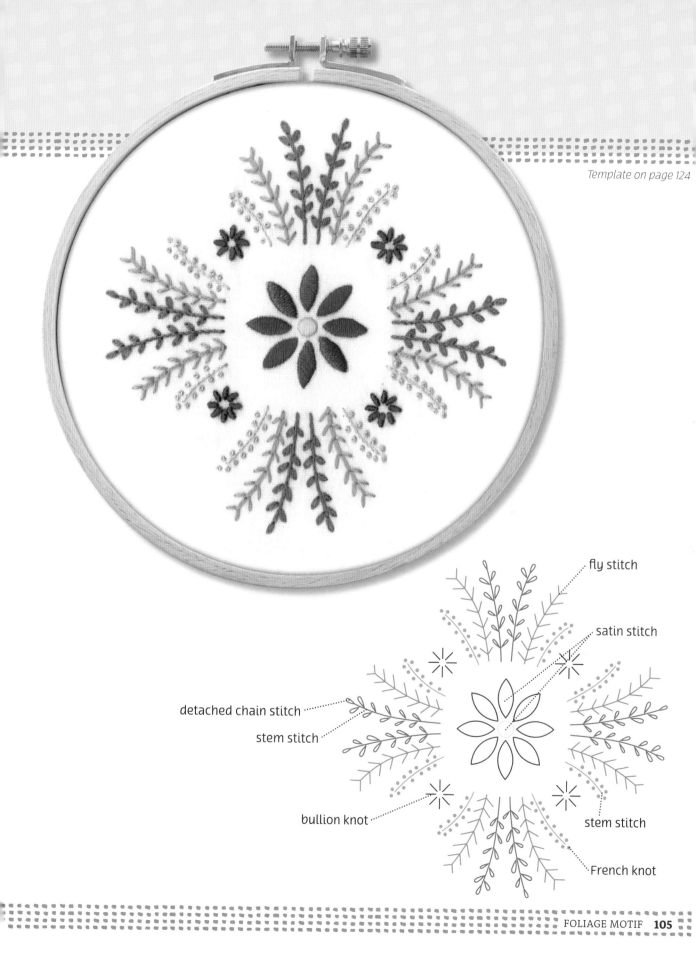

Template on page 124

fly stitch

satin stitch

detached chain stitch

stem stitch

bullion knot

stem stitch

French knot

Blue Neckline

825
Blue

Paisley shapes

Embroider the paisley shapes in satin stitch using two strands of thread. Bring your thread to the front at the pointed tip (rather than in the center) and take a small stitch up the fatter side of the paisley to determine the angle of your satin stitches. Fill the shape from there.

Teardrop collar

Fill the shapes along the top of the design in satin stitch using two strands of thread. Take your first stitch from the point to the center of the curve and embroider one half first, then the other. Embroider the lines below the teardrops and on either side of the design in stem stitch using three strands of thread.

Diamonds

Using four strands of thread, outline the upper diamond in stem stitch, the small diamond in the center in backstitch, and the cross in the middle as a four-legged knot. With three strands of thread, outline the lower diamond in stem stitch, the small diamond in the center in backstitch, and the cross in the middle as a four-legged knot. Embroider the small diamond between the upper and lower diamonds in backstitch and the cross inside as a four-legged knot, using three strands of thread.

Circles

The circles are blanket-stitch pinwheels. Use two strands of thread for the four bigger circles and one strand for the five smaller circles.

Details

Use four strands of thread for the French knots around the upper diamond and the bullion knots inside. Wrap your thread around the needle six times for the shorter bullions and nine times for the longer bullions. Use three strands of thread for the French and bullion knots of the lower diamond. Wrap your thread around the needle six times for the shorter bullions and eight times for the longer bullions. The clusters of French knots are made using two strands of thread.

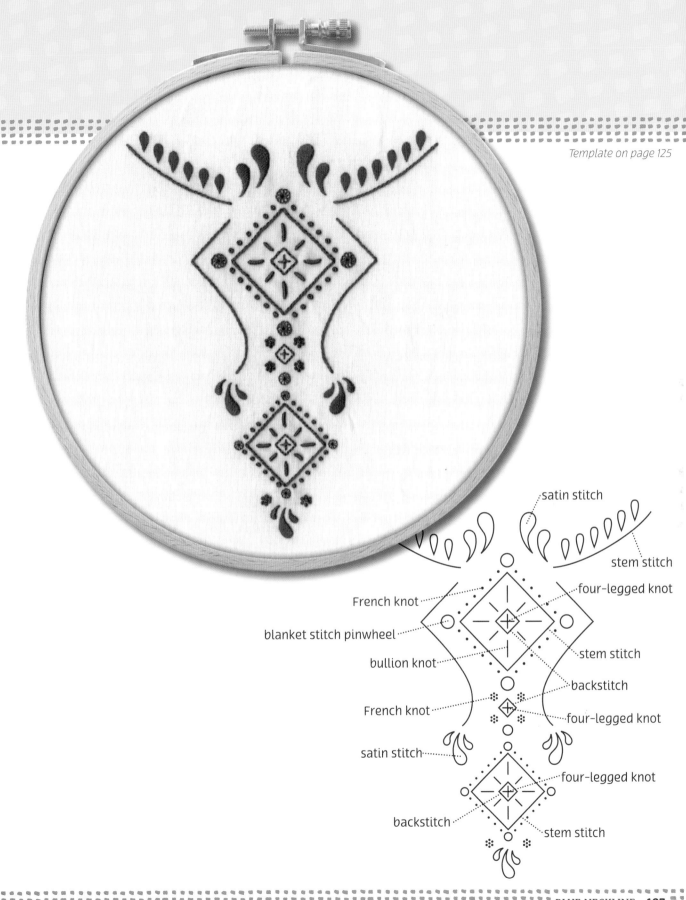

Template on page 125

satin stitch

stem stitch

French knot

four-legged knot

blanket stitch pinwheel

stem stitch

bullion knot

backstitch

French knot

four-legged knot

satin stitch

four-legged knot

backstitch

stem stitch

PROJECT 45
Elegant Monogram

Embroider the letters in stem stitch using four strands of pink. Stitch a second row of stem stitch in two strands of light pink alongside the original stitching. Follow the curves of the letters, stitching above and below to create a shadow effect.

Templates on pages 126 & 127

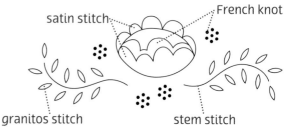

satin stitch · · · · · · · · · · · · French knot

granitos stitch · · · · · · · · · · stem stitch

PROJECT 46
Laurel Monogram

Fill the letter with rows of chain stitch using three strands of yellow. Start with a row of stitching along each of the outer edges and work toward the middle, following the shape of the letter.

detached chain stitch

stem stitch

Templates on pages 126 & 127

Floral Monogram

Embroider the letter in stem stitch using three strands of orange. For letters with points (such as A, D, I, N, L, and others) take your needle down through the fabric at the end of each letter stroke as if ending the row, secure your thread by looping it through a previous stitch on the back of your work, and then bring it up again through the same hole to start the next stroke of the letter. This gives you a nice, sharp point.

Templates on pages 114 & 126

backstitch

satin stitch

stem stitch

Grand Monogram

Fill the block letter with rows of stem stitch using four strands of yellow. Figure out how the different strokes of the letter will join up before starting the embroidery—a good rule of thumb is to replicate the way you'd write the letter. Start with the two outer rows and work toward the center for each stroke of the letter.

Embroider the script letters on either side in stem stitch using three strands of blue. Work in the same direction as you'd write the letter, embroidering over the original stitching where the strokes of the letter cross each other (as in the G).

*Templates on
pages 125, 126 & 127*

stem stitch   satin stitch

whipped chain stitch

PROJECT 49
Rustic Monogram

Embroider the letters in cable stem stitch using three strands of light green. Stitch in the same direction as you'd write the letters.

granitos stitch   fly stitch

Templates on pages 126 & 127

PROJECT 50
Romantic Monogram

Embroider the script letters in whipped chain stitch, using three strands of gray for the foundation row of chain stitching and two strands of white to whip it.

Outline the block letters in chain stitch with two strands of gray.

satin stitch

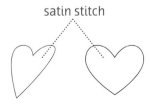

Templates on pages 126 & 127

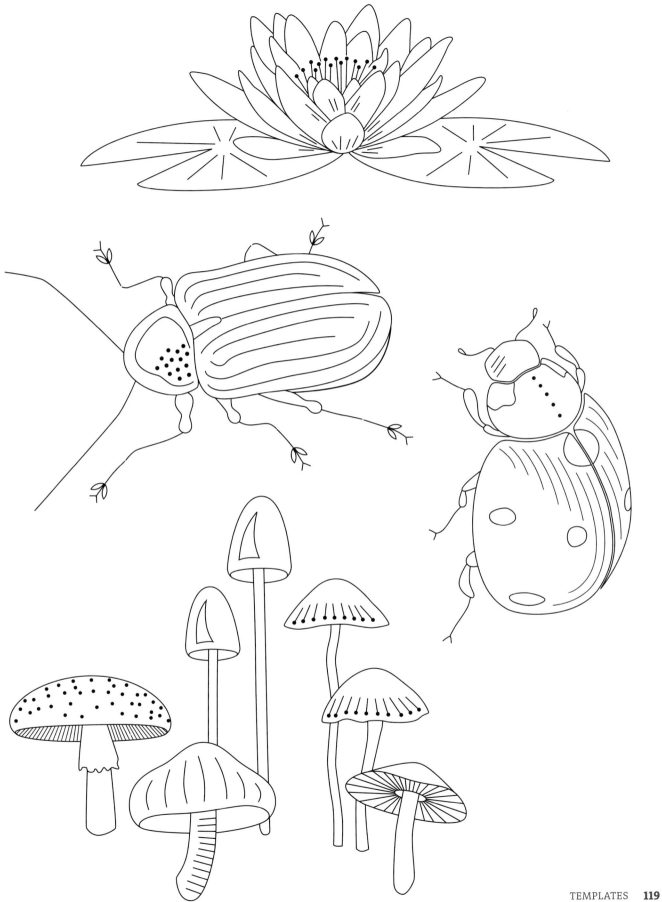

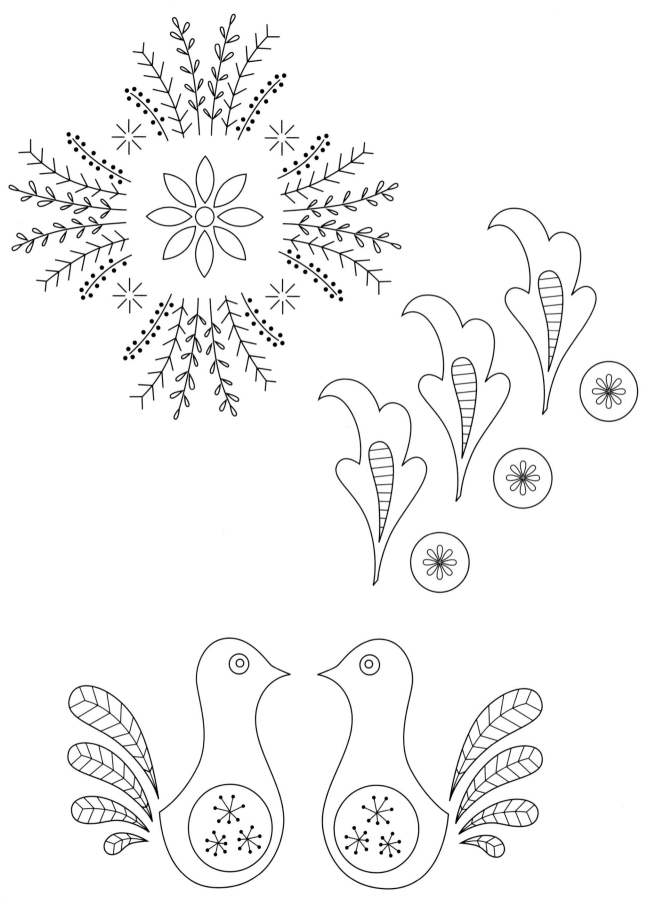

ABCDEF

GHIJKLM

NOPQRST

UVWXYZ

About the Author

Kelly Fletcher is a largely self-taught hand embroiderer who grew up with needles and thread, fabric and yarn. She creates content for magazine, book and kit publishers worldwide, designs hand embroidery patterns for her online shop and is the author of Embroidered Home, 120 Embroidery Stitches and Embroidery Tips, Tricks & Techniques. She favors creative surface embroidery with its many different stitches and puts a contemporary spin on traditional stitches and techniques to create fresh designs that appeal to modern embroiderers. Find out more at www.kellyfletcher.co.za.